Using the 1990 U.S. Census for Research

GUIDES TO MAJOR SOCIAL SCIENCE DATA BASES

EDITOR
Peter V. Marsden
Harvard University

The purpose of this series is to guide and inform about secondary use of major social science data bases. Each volume serves as a user's guide to one significant, frequently analyzed source of information, reviewing its content, study design, procedures for gaining access to the data sets, and the kinds of analyses that the data can support. The guides will also direct the prospective user to additional documentation of interest, including detailed codebooks and technical reports.

1. **The NORC General Social Survey: A User's Guide**
   James A. Davis
   Tom W. Smith

2. **The Panel Study of Income Dynamics: A User's Guide**
   Martha S. Hill

3. **Using the 1990 U.S. Census for Research**
   Richard E. Barrett

Using the 1990 U.S. Census for Research

Guides to Major Social Science Data Bases 3

Richard E. Barrett

SAGE Publications
International Educational and Professional Publisher
Thousand Oaks   London   New Delhi

For information address:

SAGE Publications, Inc.
2455 Teller Road
Thousand Oaks, California 91320

SAGE Publications Ltd.
6 Bonhill Street
London EC2A 4PU
United Kingdom

SAGE Publications India Pvt. Ltd.
M-32 Market
Greater Kailash I
New Delhi 110 048 India

Printed in the United States of America

Library of Congress Cataloging-in-Publication Data

Barrett, Richard Edward.
   Using the 1990 U.S. census for research / Richard E. Barrett.
     p.   cm. — (Guides to major social science data bases, ISSN
1058-4862 ; vol. 3)
   Includes bibliographical references.
   ISBN 0-8039-5389-5. — ISBN 0-8039-5390-9 (pbk.)
     1. United States—Census, 21st, 1990. 2. Population research—
United States.   I. Title.   II. Series: Guides to major social
science data bases ; vol. 3.
   HA201   1990ad
   304.6 ' 0973 ' 09049—dc20   94-17655

94 95 96 97 98   10 9 8 7 6 5 4 3 2 1

Sage Production Editor: Yvonne Könneker

Contents

This book is dedicated to my wife, Teresa Chou, who took time from her busy schedule to provide the author with the love, sustenance, commiseration, and unequal division of household labor that permitted its completion.

Acknowledgments

This book grew out of a conversation with Richard Campbell, who was then forced to review several parts of it. It was based on work done several years ago as a consultant for SPSS, Inc.; my colleagues there (Donald Faggiani, Mark Rodeghier, Nancy Morrison, Cathy Maahs-Fladung, and Christopher Ross) all helped me explore census data, its organization, and its uses. The puzzled looks of students in my demography classes helped me decide what researchers had to know about the census; Shufen Tseng (my teaching assistant) and Sungman Hwang were particularly helpful.

A number of scholars outside (Harvey Choldin, Moshe Semyonov, Kirk Wolter, Robert Groves, Dowell Myers, Marta Kusczak, Pini Herman, Nancy Cunniff, Barry Chiswick, Reynolds Farley, Susan Anderson, Thomas Leuthner, and Erik Austin) and inside (Robert Fay, Suzanne Bianchi, Robert Marx, Jeffrey Moore, Gregg Robinson, and Ken Taylor) the Bureau of the Census gave me good advice and useful information. None of the aforementioned are responsible for any errors contained here, of which there are undoubtedly some, or for future changes in Bureau of the Census policies and procedures that may render parts of this text obsolete or incorrect.

Series Editor's Introduction

In one way of conducting social science research, independent investigators take responsibility for all phases of a research project: After formulating ideas, they collect, analyze, and present evidence. This "holistic" approach was once the dominant style, and of course many researchers continue to follow it. In much contemporary research, however, the tasks of data collection and data analysis have come to be separated. Analysts often study information contained in large, multiuser databases assembled by major survey organizations and government agencies. These databases are designed to meet multiple purposes and tend to be of long-term value to the research community. Such large data-gathering efforts are generally conducted on a scale that is beyond the capacity of the independent researcher or the small research team; they are expensive and time-consuming.

Much, or even most, analysis of these bodies of information is done by "secondary" researchers other than those responsible for directing "primary" data collection. The separation of data collection from data analysis means, however, that users of a database must learn about its design and content as well as the research methods used in producing it. Such knowledge is essential to informed secondary analysis. Even the reader of a study based on a large-scale database may wish to know more about these matters than is provided by the brief summary description of the data typically made available in a research report.

The purpose of this series is to help to diffuse the knowledge required for informed secondary use of major social science databases. Each volume serves as a user's guide to one significant, frequently analyzed source of information, reviewing its content, study design, sampling plan, and field procedures. Each guide gives details about the various publicly available data sets produced using information available in the database, and how to gain access to them; each also illustrates the kinds of analyses that the database can support.

Finally, the guide directs the prospective user to additional documentation of interest, including detailed codebooks and technical reports.

This guide, the third in the series, is about the use of information collected in the 1990 U.S. census. Originally conducted for the purpose of apportioning seats in the House of Representatives among the states, the census has become a vital source of statistical data on many aspects of the American population. It is now used by the government in administering many laws and programs, and it has become an indispensable source of data for demographers and other social scientists. The census is especially valuable for the study of locally concentrated populations or numerically small groups, neither of which can be studied readily in typical sample surveys that include 1,500 to 3,000 observations.

Richard E. Barrett's guide reviews the history and content of the census and explains the issues that researchers using it must confront. He indicates the topics that are on the "short forms" administered to everyone and those that are measured for a sample of the population on "long forms." Barrett notes some significant changes in the 1990 census—in, for example, the measurement of ancestry, education, and relationships among household members. He reviews census definitions of geographic units, the procedures used by the Bureau of the Census to gather data, and some significant problems—notably that of undercount. The guide gives special attention to the available data products based on the 1990 census, including both data on geographic units and the Public Use Microdata Samples. Barrett identifies the different forms in which researchers can obtain these data, including printed tables, microfiche, magnetic tape, and CD-ROM. Throughout the guide, he provides detailed examples to illustrate the discussion; at the end, he directs the reader to sources of additional information about the 1990 census and data products based on it. Barrett's guide provides a cogent and accessible introduction to a rich and valuable source of information for social scientists.

—PETER V. MARSDEN, SERIES EDITOR

1. History and Current Contents of the Census

Research Questions and Census Data

The 1990 U.S. census provides a vast and wonderful array of data. This short monograph is designed to help the researcher who has a research question and wants to determine whether or not the census might be a useful source of data on this question.

More specifically, this monograph is aimed at helping users with

a. research questions or hypotheses that can be tested using census data

> *Example A.* Landale and Tolnay (1993) were interested in the degree to which ethnicity and whether one was a first- or second-generation American had an effect on age at marriage in the northern United States in the early 20th century. The Public Use Microdata Sample for the U.S. census of 1910, a household and individual-level data set, allowed them to test whether migrants and their children married later and whether ethnicity played a key role in the delay of marriage.

> *Example B.* In his influential article "American Apartheid: Segregation and the Making of the Underclass," Douglas Massey (1990) argues that "racial segregation is crucial to explaining the emergence of the urban underclass during the 1970s" (p. 329). Although his work extends Wilson's (1987) work on the same topic, Massey uses data from a file of about 21,000 census tracts (geographic units used by the Bureau of the Census with typical populations of about 2,500 to 8,000 persons) from 60 metropolitan areas to show that though the downward spiral of the quality of life in Black urban neighborhoods was influenced by national economic problems, racial segregation played a crucial role in concentrating poverty there. Both Massey's hypothetical examples of how segregation can concentrate poverty and his historical analysis of how this process occurs rely entirely on areal-level census data.

b. research questions that may use other data sources for testing hypotheses, but that need census data to flesh out additional parts of the argument

Example C. Stevens (1992) used the 1976 Survey of Income and Education to investigate the pressures and incentives that affect whether persons use a language other than English in the United States. As she points out, census data on other language use are not perfect but they do show that, in 1980, "over 23 million Americans spoke a non-English language at home" (p. 171). Here, census data show, in a relatively authoritative way, that this topic is an important one because non-English speakers continue to be a large group in U.S. society and hence are deserving of study.

c. research questions that cannot be tested statistically but for which census data can often play a vital role in providing the logical core of the empirical argument

Example D. The sociologist James Coleman is seldom thought of as a demographer; he is far better known as an educational researcher, and, more recently, as a proponent of theories of rational choice in social action. Yet in his 1992 American Sociological Association Presidential Address, the key data he presented were from the U.S. census.

Coleman (1993) wished to demonstrate that from the 18th century on, there had been a far-reaching transformation of society, and "this transformation is characterized by the decline of primordial institutions based on the family as the central element of social organization and the replacement of these institutions by purposively constructed organization" (p. 1). He demonstrated this change through the use of census data (from the United States and four other nations) on the decline in the percentage of the labor force engaged in agriculture between 1780 and 1990. These census data, which show a very similar pattern in each nation, are a powerful rhetorical device because they are repeated measures of a relatively simple concept that is known to be measured in roughly the same way in each nation. There are few other kinds of data that can be compared across time and between nations in this way.

All of these researchers did better research because they understood the use (and misuse) of census data. Understanding does not necessarily result in use. Stevens, for example, explicitly rejected the use of individual-level census data on non-English language use in favor of data from the 1976 Survey of Income and Education for her major analysis even though she recognized that census data have some uses in establishing a historical profile of national levels of non-English language use. Researchers in sociology, economics, political science, urban studies, and a number of other fields can do better work by understanding what can and cannot be done with census data.

Available Data From the 1990 Census

The 1990 Census of Population and Housing was administered in two versions, a "short form" that all households filled out and a "long form" that about one out of every six households received. Thus, in designing a research project, it is important to know which version contains the questions of interest to you. This topic will be explored in more detail later in this chapter.

Bureau of the Census policies on how 1990 census data are released will also affect a research design. Briefly, the Bureau publishes *printed data* on a variety of topics asked in the 1990 census for areal units ranging from entire states down to villages, townships, or even census tracts.

The Bureau of the Census also publishes much more extensive data on geographical units in *electronic media* (including magnetic tapes, CD-ROMs, and computer files available through on-line data services like CompuServe and DIALOG) or on *microfiche*. Because it is frequently easier to obtain and process large amounts of data from electronic media than from printed sources, it is important that the researcher have some understanding of data sources in order to estimate the amount of time, effort, and money needed to obtain and process them.

Both the printed and electronic media allow the comparisons of *populations in different areas*. As such, they are ideal for *ecological analysis*. Such areal data can also be used as the base populations (i.e., the denominators) for various kinds of rates where the numerators are taken from other sources, such as the number of events (e.g., crimes, births, etc.) occurring in the same areas in different years.

Finally, the Bureau of the Census has released two large *samples* of households (and the individuals within them) from the 1990 census on magnetic tape and CD-ROM. These samples (a 5% sample nationwide and a 1% sample of metropolitan areas) can be used to compare households and individuals, just as can be done with conventional survey data.

These *Public Use Microdata Samples* (PUMS) for the 1990 census include all of the long-form information for every individual in each sampled household. Long-form PUMS (with different sample sizes and frames) exist for every census since 1940, so that it is possible to make detailed comparisons of the changes in American society (and its various regions) over the past 50 years.

Using the PUMS from the 1980 and 1990 censuses one could, for example, compare the monetary returns to schooling for Blacks and Whites in 1980 and 1990. One could run the same regression analysis for a set of Rust Belt and Sun Belt cities in each year to see if the Black-White disparity in the relation of earnings to education has narrowed in cities with strong records of job growth, a topic of debate among urban sociologists and labor economists.

TIGER AND THE NEW
1990 CENSUS GEOGRAPHY

The 1990 census may well be remembered as much for its graphical products as for its demographic ones. Due to a concerted effort by a number of agencies, there is now an electronic map of the entire United States down to the block level. The electronic map includes physical features as well as different kinds of political and census-unit boundaries.

This mapping system, known as TIGER (Topographically Integrated Geographic Encoding and Referencing), has taken advantage of advances in computer mapping over the past two decades. The maps generated by TIGER from its very large data files (available on a variety of media) can be "printed" either on a printer or on the screen of a video display terminal.

The TIGER system becomes of more interest to social scientists because of its capability to link census data to geography in a graphical way. There are now a number of software programs that allow the user to take a census variable (percentage Black in a census tract, per capita income in a county) and to display the data in map form, or, in some cases, to display maps with two variables for the same unit (using a color scheme for one and a cross-hatching scheme for the other, etc.). A researcher can now observe the *spatial* distribution of a variable, of the residuals of a regression equation, of an observed/ expected ratio of a disease rate, and so on.

This kind of spatial representation of data has taken a huge leap forward with developments in the TIGER system. In conjunction with breakthroughs in memory capacity in personal computers and the advent of inexpensive CD-ROM readers that can be attached to PCs, there are great opportunities for geographic demography using the

1990 census. Although this monograph is not the place to discuss these advances in Geographic Information Systems (GIS), the new geographic technology may have a profound effect on how we think about a number of demographic and social problems (see Garson & Biggs, 1992).

A Brief History of the Census

The U.S. census is the world's oldest continuous census system. Censuses have been held every 10 years since 1790. Since 1790, it has been the source of information for the periodic reapportionment of seats in the U.S. House of Representatives between states, and, more recently, for the redistricting of these House seats (and other population-based legislative districts) within states, cities, and other governmental units.

U.S. census data on race and Hispanic origin are also used to redefine voting districts in accordance with the 1965 Voting Rights Act and other recent statutes and various court decisions on fair representation. The U.S. census is also a key source of data on the size of the population and on important social and economic characteristics of states and smaller localities down to the block level.

The importance of the U.S. census becomes clearer if we compare our statistical system to those of other nations. Briefly, most other nations require some form of registration of households and household members and their vital events in a registry that is available to the central government. No such household registration system exists in the United States, and there is virtually unlimited internal migration.

Because registration of vital events is controlled by local or state rather than by national authorities, the federal government has surprisingly little statutory authority or bureaucratic ability to obtain up-to-date information on a highly diverse and mobile population.

Since the time of the Great Depression and the massive mobilization of national resources for World War II, the federal government has seen the need for accurate and current information on the population. State and local governments, businesses, and private individuals and organizations also consider the federal government responsible for the collection of accurate, timely, and politically unbiased information on social and economic trends.

The federal government has tried to meet these challenges in several ways. First, it has strengthened the data collection and dissemination efforts of the decennial U.S. census. Although there have been those who have pushed for a census every 5 years, the cost and sheer human effort of conducting a census of population and housing has led most observers to predict that a shift to a shorter interval between censuses is not likely soon. Instead, the Bureau of the Census appears to be concentrating on expanding the availability of its data products from the decennial census and on refining its sample survey products (see below).

Second, in addition to the Census of Population and Housing (the major topic of this monograph), the federal government conducts separate censuses of economic activity, covering agriculture, manufacturing, mineral industries, transportation, governments, construction, retail trade, wholesale trade, and service industries. These are censuses of *establishments* rather than of individuals or households and provide extensive data on revenues, payrolls, employment, size of establishment, and other topics. These censuses are held in years ending in 2 or 7, and the data are available for different geographic units in both printed and electronic form.

The data from these economic censuses can be cross-classified with information from the decennial Census of Population and Housing. For example, companies conducting studies of store location might use the 1987 Census of Retail Trade and the 1990 census to see if the population of a town is being underserved or overserved (in terms of the ratio of stores to population) by competitors already in the area.

Third, during the years between censuses the Bureau of the Census and other federal agencies administer a variety of very large-scale national probability surveys (including the well-known *Current Population Survey*) and interfile these surveys with census data as the raw materials for the construction of various kinds of social indicators and population estimates and projections. One of these surveys, the *Survey of Income and Program Participation*, is a very large-scale panel study that is becoming a major source of data for social scientists, both by itself and in conjunction with other census and survey data.

Because the census is conducted only once every 10 years, and because many major trends (such as business cycles) occur at more frequent intervals, surveys are a key adjunct to census data collection efforts. For example, the "baby boom" in the United States began about 1947 and lasted until about 1957, after which birth rates began a long, slow decline (Moore & O'Connell, 1978). If school planners only had the 1940 and 1950 censuses to rely on in projecting school enrollment in the early 1960s then they might have overestimated the number of elementary school classrooms needed in the late 1960s.

More recently, Current Population Survey (CPS) data have shown that there are remarkable turnarounds in regional growth and migration rates between the early and late 1980s. The Midwest has quadrupled its rate of population growth since 1985, and the West South Central Division (Arkansas, Louisiana, Texas, and Oklahoma) changed from having the highest rate of net in-migration to the highest rate of net out-migration between 1981 and 1987 (U.S. Bureau of the Census, 1992g, p. iii). Up-to-date annual survey data help to chart the rapidly changing social and economic trends that the decennial census may miss.

Fourth, agencies of the U.S. government have developed a number of specialized databases on different parts of the population, some of which can provide longitudinal data and some of which can provide useful data beyond the narrow bureaucratic purposes for which they were developed. For example, the U.S. Bureau of the Census uses data on matched tax returns for the same individuals from different years (provided by the Internal Revenue Service) to estimate internal migration rates in the United States. The Social Security Administration uses data from its files together with National Center for Health Statistics mortality data to develop estimates of future life spans and length of working life (see Raymondo, 1992, pp. 94-97). There are, however, often major legal, bureaucratic, and technical barriers to outside researchers who might want to use these data sets. Privacy laws and other government regulations often make it difficult to obtain such data.

WHAT IS A CENSUS?

A modern census has four key elements (Yaukey, 1985, pp. 17-19). It should be universal: Everyone in the census area should be enumerated. It should be simultaneous: Everyone should be counted at the same time to minimize the number of those who might be missed (underenumeration) or double-counted (overenumeration) if a census is extended over a long period of time. It should be periodic: Everyone should be counted at regular intervals in order to permit measurement of changes in the population. Finally, a census should be individual: The enumeration of each person should include different descriptive variables about that person (age, sex, etc.) so that individual-level variables can be cross-classified.

The U.S. census has had to make several adjustments of these general principles in attempting to count a highly mobile population at minimum cost (recent survey work by the Bureau of the Census indicates that "about 18 percent of the nation's householders moved into their homes within the previous 12-month period"; U.S. General Accounting Office, 1992, p. 47). The principle of *universality* is still held in high regard by the Bureau of the Census, but it is recognized that certain groups, such as the homeless or minority males in poverty areas, are particularly prone to underenumeration.

The Bureau of the Census attempted to achieve a simultaneous count by having the U.S. Postal Service deliver all census forms to the correct addresses shortly before April 1, 1990, and by requesting that recipients return the completed forms in postage-paid envelopes before April 1. The U.S. census is a *de facto* census: that is, it attempts to measure people in terms of where they actually live on April 1, rather than where they officially live (as is done in the *de jure* censuses used in a number of other nations). Yet mailed-in census forms were often completed on some date after April 1 or respondents were interviewed by census takers after that date, so there is some question as to whether respondents were referring to the population of their households as of April 1.

The U.S. census is stronger in the area of counting *individuals* and in its *periodic* nature. The census has been held every 10 years since 1790, and censuses since 1850 have recorded individual-level data (Anderson, 1988, pp. 32-44). The census also has a long tradition of building cross-tabulated tables for individuals even in small areal units.

Since 1940, the U.S. census has been a census of *population* and *housing*. Census forms are mailed out (or interviewers are dispatched) to residential addresses, and the census questionnaire includes questions about both the condition of the housing unit and about its occupants.

There is no reason why a nation could not conduct separate censuses of population and housing. In China, a nation with a household registration system, censuses of population were carried out in 1982 and 1990, and a separate census of housing was carried out in 1985 (see Ministry of Construction, 1986). In the United States, where no household or individual registration system exists, it makes much more sense to conduct censuses of housing and population together, because the counting of all residences in the nation is one of the few ways of ascertaining that the entire population was counted.

Although the *individual* is the key building block of many census tabulations, it is important to note that the census form itself is not filled out by every person in each residence. Instead, the Bureau of the Census asks one person in the household to fill out the census questionnaire and to provide information on all of the persons living at that address. As will be noted later, there are possibilities of error in the reporting of some data on household members by the census respondent.

The *periodic* nature of the U.S. census means that most of the population has experienced a census before. The periodic decennial nature of the U.S. census also has a great benefit for data users. Because the data are collected as of April 1 of each decennial census year, and are also frequently available in estimated form for June 30—the midpoint of the census year—as well, it makes it easy to compute rates of change. In China, on the other hand, censuses were conducted in 1953, 1964 (11 years later), 1982 (18 years later), and 1990 (8 years later). Computing census-based annual rates of change for different variables takes far longer with Chinese than with U.S. data, where there is a standard 10-year interval.

COMPLIANCE WITH THE CENSUS

In many less developed and some developed nations there is such a deep-seated distrust of the central government in some localities that any attempt to conduct a census would meet with massive noncompliance.

The question of noncompliance might be thought of in two ways: individual and group. Undoubtedly there are a number of people who are hiding out from government agencies, abusive spouses or other individuals or groups who do not want to be found, and who are unlikely to fill out their census forms.

Group noncompliance, that is, an organized effort to avoid being counted by the census, would be a much more serious problem (and source of bias) for the Bureau of the Census. Fortunately, there appears to have been little organized effort by any group to avoid being counted in recent censuses. The very high undercount rates of Native Americans on reservations (12.2% were missed in 1990, according to the Post-Enumeration Survey; see Hogan, 1993, p. 1054) may be at least partially due to suspicion of the U.S. government among this group, however.

Although the Bureau of the Census stresses that individuals' answers to census questions are kept confidential, there have been negative repercussions for some groups in the past due to the use of areal data. During World War II, the Bureau of the Census provided the War Relocation Agency with detailed counts of the number of Japanese Americans for small areal units of the United States from the 1940 census. This information helped the U.S. government to round up citizens and noncitizens of Japanese ancestry and to ship them to internment camps for much of the war. Although the Bureau of the Census did not provide individual-level data, its small-area counts helped the government carry out what has later been acknowledged as a gross violation of the civil rights of this group (see Anderson, 1988, pp. 193-194).

It is also difficult to conceive of the U.S. census as a source for military data. Yet the 1860 census provided important information on livestock, crop production, number of free Blacks, slaves, Whites, and a host of other topics on Georgia counties to General William Tecumseh Sherman during his famous March to the Sea in 1864 (Anderson, 1988, p. 64).

Even with the publicity that preceded the 1990 census, a Bureau of the Census survey showed that on Census Day (April 1, 1990), only 94.9% of all non-Hispanic Whites and between 80.6% and 90.4% of all minority groups had heard of the census. Further, a National Opinion Research Center survey showed that those who felt that the census was not important to the country or to their own community were more than twice as likely to fail to mail back their census forms as those who saw a useful purpose in the census (Eriksen, Estrada, Tukey, & Wolter, 1991, pp. 70-72). Declining levels of awareness of or belief in the importance of the census appear to be having a major effect on overall rates of compliance and will be a major factor in determining the ways in which the year 2000 census is redesigned (see U.S. General Accounting Office, 1992, pp. 35-41).

GOVERNANCE AND ADMINISTRATION OF THE CENSUS

Throughout its long history, the Bureau of the Census has tried to strike a balance in its questionnaire construction. It has tried to:

a. ask questions that are at least somewhat comparable to those asked in prior censuses, so that broad changes in the demographic parameters of the population can be ascertained (Scott, 1968, pp. 121-122). For example, from 1850 on, the census has asked "place of birth" so that the relative impact of international migration versus natural increase (i.e., births minus deaths) in each intercensal decade can be measured.

b. ask some questions that are of current interest, so that lawmakers (who provide the funding) and others will see the census as providing useful information to themselves and their constituents. For example, the more extensive delineation of both Hispanic and Asian and Pacific Islander groups (i.e., in numerous subcategories) since 1980 was due to a perceived need for a better understanding of the different social and economic positions of these smaller groups, as well as to effective lobbying by these groups.

c. ask questions that persons will answer; that is, ask questions that will not be seen as an invasion of privacy, and ask them in such a way that persons will give meaningful answers.

Historically, the attempt to balance these competing purposes and pressures has meant that many different kinds of questions have been used in different censuses. The 1790 census only asked three questions (color, free or slave, and sex for free White persons only), but by 1860 there were 142 items spread across six different questionnaires. In 1880, there were 13,010 different items of information collected on different schedules (Kaplan, Van Valey, & Associates, 1980, pp. 10-16).

Since 1902, when the Bureau of the Census was established, and particularly since 1930, when the Bureau staff began to be able to write questions with less outside interference, the particularly intrusive census questions (e.g., on insanity, criminal record, amount of debts, etc.) began to disappear from the schedule (Halacy, 1980, pp. 138-143).

The questions for the 1990 census were written by Bureau of the Census staff under the authority of Title 13 of the United States Code. Their questions were reviewed by the Director of the Bureau of the Census and also by the Office of Management of the Budget. In addition, 3 years before the census, the U.S. Congress must be advised of the proposed topics of investigation, and 2 years before the census the Congress must be given the wording of the questions to be asked (U.S. Bureau of the Census, 1992e, p. 9).

Although the Bureau of the Census has the responsibility for deciding questions for each new census, it solicits considerable input from outside groups before such decisions are made. During 1984 and 1985, Bureau of the Census administrators and representatives of state and local organizations met in Local Public Meetings throughout the United States to get input on local data needs. Ethnic groups and minority groups were consulted about the content and wording of questions. Other federal agencies were also polled as to their data needs (U.S. Bureau of the Census, 1992e, p. 7).

This kind of input allows the Bureau of the Census to ascertain which questions in prior censuses were not very useful and might be eliminated. For example, the 1980 questions on marital history, carpooling, and weeks spent looking for work in the previous year apparently were of little use to researchers or local planners and were dropped in 1990. Nowadays, questions on such topics may require very detailed answers to produce usable results, and a detailed survey like the Current Population Survey may be a much better vehicle than the census for getting at this information.

These meetings, telephone calls, letters, and so on also help the Bureau of the Census decide the levels of aggregation at which various data should be made available. Even with the recent revolution in electronic data retrieval, it is still a truism that the smaller the areal unit, the less detailed the census information that is available. Localities are now, however, frequently required to use detailed census data to meet statutory requirements. For example, in the process of legislative reapportionment, localities were required to use data on race and Spanish/Hispanic origin at the block level, so the Bureau of the Census had to supply such information to them (in the Public Law 94-171 compilations, the first local area data released from the 1990 census).

Statutory requirements, Bureau of the Census traditions, levels of constituent interest, and cost factors all influence the choices the Bureau makes with regard to what *media* are chosen for data publication. If data are of general interest and receive frequent use by nonspecialists, they will be produced in printed form. If data are primarily of interest to specialists or are very lengthy, they will be produced in another medium: on magnetic tape, CD-ROM, or microfiche, or sometimes in more than one form.

Questions that have never appeared on the U.S. census can also tell us about the relationship of the American population to its government. For example, despite considerable pressure, the Bureau of the Census has never had a required item on religion on the Census of Population (although special surveys on church membership were conducted in conjunction with it between 1850 and 1890 and in Censuses of Religious Bodies from 1905 to 1936; see Halacy, 1980, p. 83).

In 1957 the Bureau of the Census's Current Population Survey included a question on religion. This resulted in opposition from Jewish groups and from Christian Scientists, and the question has not been repeated (Starr, 1987, pp. 41-42). A proposal to add a religion question on the 1970 census encountered widespread opposition from those who opposed it as an invasion of privacy or as likely to lead to decreased compliance with the census by some parts of the population (Scott, 1968, pp. 122-123). A recent revision of Title 13 of the United States Code (Public Law 94-521 of 1976) specifically forbids the census from requiring that any person disclose religious belief or affiliation in the census (Halacy, 1980, p. 226).

As a result, Bogue's (1985) study of the demography of religious affiliation in the United States, one of the few such studies available, relies heavily on data from the National Opinion Research Center's General Social Survey (pp. 645-663). By way of contrast, 13 out of 19 censuses in Asian and Pacific nations conducted from 1976 to 1981 list religion as a questionnaire item (Cho & Hearn, 1984, p. xvii).

Another item that has not been included on the population questionnaire is the respondent's Social Security number. Requiring the Social Security number could provide useful information that could be used in estimating the census undercount, linking census data to other administrative records to estimate migration and error rates, and so on. After a debate on the topic prior to the 1970 census (Scott, 1968, pp. 123-124), however, it apparently was not pursued in a serious fashion for the 1980 or 1990 censuses. Privacy issues and the possibility of decreasing compliance may have prevented the inclusion of this item. A 1992 test using a simplified census questionnaire showed that including a question requesting the respondent's Social Security number decreased the response rate by about 5% to 10% (Bates, 1993).

Changes in the Census Questionnaire
Between 1980 and 1990

One aspect of census design of concern to many researchers is that the topics covered and even the questions on the same topic change from one census to the next. Numerous authors (Alonso & Starr, 1987; Anderson, 1988; Halacy, 1980) have pointed out that the census, both in the questions asked and the kinds of tabular and analytic work later provided, is a mirror of many of the concerns of the nation—and the influence of different political groups—at that time. The questions asked, the degree of specificity of those questions (such as the much greater attention to Asian and Pacific Islander racial groups in the 1980 and 1990 censuses), and whether the question is asked on the complete or sample count questionnaire can differ from census to census.

Many census researchers eventually use data from at least one prior census as well. Census data from one year are often less conclusive than is first imagined. Once one shows that Blacks' household incomes are lower than Whites' in 1990, an obvious next question is whether this income gap is shrinking or widening. An examination of 1990 and 1980 census data on this topic is often the only way to investigate this problem.

Of course, it is crucial to know whether the concepts of income, household, and race were defined the same way in 1980 as in 1990. Chart 1.1 gives a brief introduction to this question of comparability of census questions over time.

Researchers are urged to investigate early on in the research design phase of their project whether (a) similar questions were asked in each census year, (b) the answers were coded in the same way, and (c) the data are available for similar census geographic units or for individuals, families, or households in each census year.

In the following section, some of the major changes between the 1980 and 1990 census questionnaires and their implications for research will be discussed. Because most researchers will be interested in particular *topic areas*, that approach will be used in discussing these changes. Researchers may also wish to consult with the Association of Public Data Users' (APDU) *Census Comparability Project*, which examines changing concepts of income, race, household structure, and so on, between decennial censuses, and to look at the *Glossary* (U.S. Bureau of the Census, 1993c, pp. 19-66) for other information on comparability.

CHANGING CONCEPTS OF HOUSEHOLDS AND HOUSEHOLD RELATIONSHIPS

Both the 1980 and 1990 censuses retained the same overall format: One individual living in the household was supposed to fill out all information for all coresident persons in that household. The first

CHART 1.1. Topics Covered in the 1990 Census Questionnaire, With 1980 Comparisons

---

Topics Covered in the 100% Component

Population Questions	*Housing Questions*
Household relationship (2)*	Number of units in structure (H2)*
Sex (3)	Number of rooms in unit (H3)
Race (4)	Tenure—owned or rented (H4)*
Age (5)*	Value of home or monthly rent (H6)*
Marital status (6)	Congregate housing (meals included in rent) (H7b)*#
Hispanic origin (7)*	Vacancy characteristics*

Topics Covered in the Sample Component

Population Questions

Housing Questions

Social characteristics

Education—enrollment and attainment (11, 12)*

Place of birth, citizenship, and year of entry to the U.S. (8, 9, 10)*

Ancestry/ethnic origin (13)*

Migration (residence in 1985) (14)*

Language spoken at home (15)

Work disability (18)

Functional disability (19)#

Veteran status (17a, 17b)*/years of active duty (17c)#

Fertility (20)

Year moved into residence (H8)*

Number of bedrooms (H9)*

Plumbing and kitchen facilities (H10, H11)*

Telephone in unit (H12)*

Vehicles available (H13)*

Heating fuel (H14)*

Source of water and method of sewage disposal (H15, H16)

Year structure built (H17)*

Condominium status (H18)*

Farm residence (H19b)*

Shelter costs, including utilities (H20-H26)*#

Economic characteristics

Labor force (21)

Place of work (22) and journey to work (23, 24)*

Industry (28), occupation (29), and class of worker (30)*

Work experience in 1989 (31)*

Sources of income in 1989 (32)*

Year last worked (27)

NOTES: For a useful comparison of the 1980 and 1990 census questionnaires, see American Demographics staff (1989, pp. 24-31). A comparison of the 1970 and 1980 census questionnaires can be found in Kaplan et al. (1980, p. 9). A schematic presentation of topics covered in U.S. censuses between 1790 and 1970 is in Kaplan et al. (1980, pp. 434-443).

The number after each topic is the question number on the 1990 census questionnaire; numbers alone refer to the population schedule, numbers preceded by an "H" are found on the housing schedule (the 100% and sample components both have population and housing components).

* Indicates that although the question was also asked in the 1980 census questionnaire, either the question is worded differently in 1990 or response categories have been added or changed.

# Indicates that the question is new in 1990.

person listed was to be the person in whose name the residence was owned or rented, and the household relationships of all other coresident persons to this first person were to be specified. Neither the 1980 nor 1990 census used the concept of "household head."

The 1980 and 1990 censuses use different categories of household relationships. The 1980 census questionnaire gave the following categories of relatives (of the first person listed): husband/wife, son/daughter, brother/sister, father/mother, and other relative (to be written in). In the 1990 census these categories were retained, but the son/daughter category was changed to "natural-born or adopted son/daughter," and two new categories were added: stepson/stepdaughter, and grandchild.

One of the problems with using 1980 census data is that it was difficult to match the census categories with the increasing complexity of American family relationships. Although American families are not growing any larger, the decline in the proportion married and the high divorce rate of couples with children often results in a wide variety of non- and postmarital child-care arrangements (see Sweet & Bumpass, 1987, pp. 262-293; Cherlin, 1991b). The new categories should enable us to see who's minding the kids (in a residential sense, at least) to a much greater extent than the 1980 census could.

The distribution of children across family and household types is of more than just academic interest. Since 1979 there has been a surge in poverty among America's children. In 1990 the poverty rate of children under 18 years was 19.9%, and they comprised 40% of all of the nation's poor (U.S. Bureau of the Census, 1992c, p. 14). Yet relatively little demographic research has been done on the kinds of households where these poor children reside (i.e., their relationships to their primary caregivers) or to the spatial distribution of these households. The 1990 census allows us to measure some of these aspects of household organization, poverty, and spatial distribution in local areas for the first time.

The 1990 census also includes more extensive questions on *nonrelatives* (at least, those unrelated to Person No. 1 of the questionnaire). In 1980 the possible categories of nonrelated persons in the household were: roomer, boarder; partner, roommate; paid employee; and other nonrelative (to be written in). In 1990 the first category was changed to "roomer, boarder or foster child." In 1980, it was often not clear whether foster children should be listed as relatives or as unrelated persons; this category specifies their status.

The 1990 questionnaire also separates 1980's "partner, roommate" category into "housemate, roommate" and "unmarried partner." Thus the 1990 questionnaire attempts to specify who is *living together* as opposed to simply rooming together. The Bureau of the Census and other scholars estimate that several million unmarried persons are living together, but the wording of the 1980 census made it difficult to separate them from those with more transitory relationships.

CONCEPTS OF RACE, ETHNICITY, AND NATIONAL ORIGIN: SOME STABILITY

The race question is the same in 1990 as in 1980; the only change here was a more logical arrangement of the categories and a better specification of what American Indian tribe or "other" Asian-Pacific Islander group could be written in. The race question still includes the classification "Black or Negro"; although some thought was given to using the increasingly common terms *Afro-American* or *African American*, these requests came so late that it would have been very expensive to change the questionnaire.

Similarly, the "Spanish/Hispanic origin" question remained the same between 1980 and 1990; the only major change was that "other" Spanish/Hispanic groups were now supposed to write in their group. The 1990 examples of what group might be written in include a Caribbean group (Dominican) and a European one (Spaniard) in order to resolve any conceptual difficulties over what constitutes a person of Spanish/Hispanic origin.

By and large, the data on race and Hispanic origin are comparable between the last two censuses. Yet, because a surprisingly large proportion of the population is of mixed racial and Hispanic origin, the self-identification data for individuals may change considerably between censuses (Passel, 1993).

For example, the number of inhabitants of the state of Alabama reporting themselves as American Indian, Eskimo, or Aleut (the combined racial category) rose from 9,239 in 1980 to 16,506 in 1990, an increase of 78.7%. The total population of the state only rose by 3.8% during this decade. It is highly unlikely that the extraordinary increase in the size of the American Indian population was due primarily to high fertility or in-migration. Passel estimates that "more than half the growth of the American Indian population in 1960-1990 is attributed to nondemographic factors; that is, because individuals changed racial identification over time" (Passel, 1993, p. 1076).

Race and Spanish/Hispanic origin touch on only two of the many interesting questions related to social differentiation in the United States. Place of birth, citizenship, and year of entry into the United States are all asked on the sample component of the 1980 and 1990 censuses, but in slightly different ways.

In 1980 the questionnaire asked for the state where the person's mother was living as the state of birth; the 1990 form simply asks for the U.S. state or foreign country of birth. The 1980 questionnaire asks if the person is a naturalized citizen of the United States *only* if the person was born in a foreign country. The 1990 form is considerably clearer. It asks if this person is a citizen of the United States, then gives various categories: born in the United States, born in Puerto Rico or other territories, born abroad of American parents, U.S. citizen by naturalization, or not a citizen of the United States. In the 1980 form there was some possibility for misclassification of U.S. citizens born in U.S. territories (see Question No. 11, long form).

Researchers should also be aware that the Bureau of the Census administered slightly different versions of the 1990 questionnaire in Puerto Rico and in the other U.S. possessions (Guam, the U.S. Virgin Islands, and the Northern Mariana Islands). In the general U.S. questionnaire, respondents born in these U.S. possessions are directed to answer Question No. 10 ("When did this person come to the United States to stay?"), but in these special questionnaires, such an answer is not required.

The international migration question (when did this person come to the United States to stay?) is similar in 1980 and 1990, except that the 1990 question gives a finer subdivision for the 1980s (four categories) while retaining all of the 1980 form's time categories. The ability to match migration year categories for the 1980 and 1990 questionnaires should be a boon to research on international migration and its effect on occupational attainment and income because it will be possible to match similar groups of people (such as Koreans who migrated to the United States between 1970 and 1974) in two successive censuses.

The 1980 ancestry question (No. 14, "What is this person's ancestry?") was broadened in 1990 to "What is this person's ancestry or ethnic origin?" (No. 13). How this change in wording may change the *distribution* of responses is not clear.

The questions on language spoken at home by this person (Nos. 15a and 15b) and how well the person speaks English (No. 15c) remained the same between the censuses. Differences in coding procedures for these language questions between the 1980 and 1990 censuses, however, may create problems of comparability of data (see any state's *CPH-5 Summary Social, Economic, and Housing Characteristics* volume [U.S. Bureau of the Census, 1992i], Appendix B: Definitions of Subject Characteristics, subject heading "Language Spoken at Home and Ability to Speak English" for details on language groups, rules on what language was assigned to households from individual data, intercensal changes, etc.).

There was more international in-migration in the 1981-1990 decade (about 7.3 million people; see U.S. Bureau of the Census, 1992h, p. 11) than in any decade since 1941-1950 (see Bogue, 1985, p. 353; U.S. Bureau of the Census, 1975, pp. 105-109). In addition, these new migrants frequently come from nations with few cultural or linguistic linkages with the United States, so the meaning or interpretation of questions about language ability may be different than for migrants from nations with Indo-European language roots.

These census questions about place of birth, ancestry, language use, place of residence, citizenship, and so on may give us important clues about the increasingly complex world of the international migrant. Do overseas Chinese who lived for several generations in Vietnam before coming to the United States in the 1970s put down their race and ancestry/ethnic origin as Chinese, or do they use Vietnamese for race and Chinese for ancestry/ethnic origin, or vice versa? Are Asian Indians from India or Asian Indians from East Africa (who comprise a significant part of all Asian Indians in the United States) more likely to use English at home, become citizens more rapidly, and so on?

These and similar questions can be explored using the 1990 census, and, because the questions were largely similar on the 1980 census (although many of the migrant groups were much smaller then), the answers can be compared with earlier data to see how the migrants and the social system have changed over time. The 1990 census data on race, Spanish/Hispanic status, ancestry/ethnicity, language use, and year of migration provide an excellent opportunity to extend the work of such scholars as Stanley Lieberson, Reynolds Farley, Barry Chiswick, and Suzanne Model.

CHANGING CONCEPTS OF EDUCATION, OCCUPATION, AND INDUSTRY

The census has always been one of the key sources of information on the *human capital* of the United States. A question on school attendance has been asked on every census since 1850, and on educational attainment since 1940. Questions on industry of worker (in 1820, 1840, and every census since 1910), occupation (all censuses since 1850), class of worker (all censuses since 1910), and employment status (all censuses since 1930) have attempted to further refine the portrait of the U.S. workforce (Kaplan et al., 1980, pp. 436-437). A variety of questions on duration of unemployment, number of weeks worked in the last year or hours worked in the last week, and industry or occupation 5 years ago have attempted to measure degree of workforce attachment and the changing nature of employment.

The 1990 education questions attempt to measure two things: the number of persons currently enrolled in various kinds of schools and the educational attainment of the population as a whole. Question No. 11 asks if "At any time since February 1, 1990, has this person attended regular school or college?" This question uses a similar time frame to that of the 1980 census question. There was also a minor change in the response categories: "yes, public school, public college" is the same in both censuses, but the two 1980 categories "yes, private, church-related" and "yes, private, not church-related" were combined into "yes, private school, private college" in the 1990 census form.

A more significant change was made in the *educational attainment* question. National censuses often ask questions about educational attainment and less frequently about *educational qualifications* (see Cho & Hearn, 1984, p. xviii). In 1980 the U.S. census only asked about educational attainment, and asked the question in such a way that it measured highest year of school *attended* ("What is the highest grade (or year) of regular school that this person has ever attended?"). The next question, however, asked whether the person finished this grade or year of school, so a measure of completed years of schooling could be obtained.

Two other points about the 1980 education questions are worth mentioning. These questions were asked of the 100% sample, so educational statistics are available for the whole population in 1980. The response categories for years of school attended were single-year categories, starting with nursery school and including up to "8 or more" years of college.

In 1990 the education questions were shifted to the long (sample) form of the census, so the educational characteristics of local areas will be more difficult to specify. The 1990 question on educational attainment is also a more complex mix of categories that measure years of school attended and educational qualifications (i.e., degrees or diplomas) obtained. This set of mixed response categories was obtained by compressing the individual school years at some levels (primary school is now only divided into two categories, first through fourth grade and fifth through eighth grade) and by adding diploma or degree classifications.

For example, the respondent is given the choice of "12th grade, NO DIPLOMA" (emphasis in the original text) or "HIGH SCHOOL GRADUATE—high school DIPLOMA or the equivalent (for example: GED)." Given the importance of a high school diploma in the labor market, and the distressing frequency with which students can attend 12 years of school and yet not accumulate sufficient credits to get a high school diploma, this attempt to measure the educational quali-fications of the population is probably a worthwhile endeavor. The question is, to what extent can 1980 measures of educational attain-ment be compared with the 1990 version?

The 1990 classification of education has a much finer delineation of college attendance (occupational vs. academic programs) and of degrees obtained (associate, bachelor's, master's, professional, and doctoral). These data should permit far more sophisticated analyses of education, both as an independent and dependent variable. Of course, there are some trade-offs here.

One problem with 1990 census data is that it will be increasingly difficult to justify the use of global, interval measures of education (i.e., "total years of education completed") as the unit of measure. The only single-year measures are nursery school, kindergarten, and Grades 9 through 12; Grades 1 through 4 and 5 through 8 have no single-year grade categories.

The use of such broad age categories will increase measurement error. For many interesting groups, such as recent migrants from Mexico, the use of such broad schooling categories at lower levels may mask significant associations. Mexican migrants with eighth grade educations probably earn more than those with fifth grade educations, but this can no longer be determined from 1990 census data (Barry Chiswick, personal communication, March 12, 1993).

At the other end of the educational spectrum, after 12th grade, there is now no measure of *years of school attended*. This means that researchers who could have easily computed an interval measure of school attendance from the 1980 census data (i.e., by adding the number of years spent in elementary through high school to years spent in college) now have to deal with two problems.

For high school graduates, it is unknown how many years past the usual 12 it may have taken them to graduate; because the Bureau of the Census includes GED recipients here, it may have been a considerable (or worse, a highly variable) number of years. Actually, the GED recipient problem is not a new one; in 1980 they were simply told to mark down 12 years of schooling.

All we know about persons who went to college is that they either have "some college but no degree" or a specific degree, not how long it took them to obtain that sheepskin. This problem is compounded by the tendency of many American college students to extend their college years. In many large urban colleges and universities, fewer than 10% of all students graduate in 4 years or less; most cohorts only begin to graduate in large numbers in years five and six. Perhaps this is only fitting; after all, the Latin root of education is *educare*, meaning "to draw out." The former strategy of estimating annual equivalencies for college (4 years) and graduate school (2 years for an MA, 3 years for a law degree, etc.) to create an interval-level education variable is now at variance with the realities of that system.

The census questions on labor force participation, occupation, and industry changed far less between 1980 and 1990 than the education questions. The questions about labor force participation during the past week (whether the person worked and how many hours the person worked) are the same as in 1980. The question on location of employment is similar in 1980 and 1990.

There were minor changes in the journey-to-work questions between 1980 and 1990: A few transport categories were changed (and "ferryboat" was added), the 1980 question on whether a person drove alone or shared a car with others was dropped, and the time of leaving home to go to work was added. The questions on temporary layoff, whether the person has been looking for work, and when the person last worked are the same in both censuses.

Similarly, the questions on current or most recent industry, employer, and occupation are the same in 1990 as in 1980. Because these questions are widely used by many researchers, this is an important continuity between censuses.

There are two major changes in the coding of *industry* between 1980 and 1990. In 1990 U.S. military personnel can specify their service branch under "industry or employer" and their military occupation in the occupation question; in 1980, neither could be specified.

The Bureau of the Census classifies all industries into 235 industrial categories (U.S. Bureau of the Census, 1992f, pp. I-30–I-36). Researchers should be aware that like other government agencies, the Bureau of the Census uses the Office of the Management of the Budget's (OMB) 1987 Standard Industrial Classification (SIC) as a guide to its classification of industries. There are, however, significant differences between the OMB's most recent SIC code revisions (1987) and the categories used by the Bureau of the Census in 1990, just as there were between the codes used in the 1980 census and the prior versions of the OMB's SIC codes (revised in 1972 and 1977).

Some researchers will be concerned with the differences between the 1987 OMB SIC codes and the 1990 census industrial codes; however, these are well documented (see U.S. Bureau of the Census, 1992f, pp. I-30–I-36). The other problem is how the industrial classification codes have changed between censuses.

The changes in industry classifications between the 1970 and 1980 censuses are described in a technical paper (U.S. Bureau of the Census, 1989). Similar changes between the 1980 and 1990 censuses are given in a five-page document prepared by the Labor Force Statistics Branch of the Population Division (U.S. Bureau of the Census, 1993b). Further analysis of changes in intercensal industrial classification will probably be published by this branch in the future.

The Bureau of the Census's occupational classification scheme for the 1990 census generally follows the Office of Management of the Budget's Standard Occupational Classification (SOC) system. The latest revision of OMB's SOC system was in 1980; all census responses to the occupational questions (i.e., what kind of work it was and what were the most important duties of the job) are coded among about 500 occupational categories. Lists of the 1980 SOC codes can be found in the documentation for the 1980 PUMS (U.S. Bureau of the Census, 1983), and for the 1990 codes, in the documentation for the 1990 PUMS (U.S. Bureau of the Census, 1992f). The two sources mentioned above for comparisons of the SIC codes used in the 1970, 1980, and 1990 censuses (U.S. Bureau of the Census, 1989, 1993b) also include comparisons of the SOC codes used in these censuses.

For both the SIC and SOC systems the Bureau of the Census also has developed nonoverlapping categories of industry and occupation that permit standardized comparisons of broader segments of these variables. Respondents can be classified as to whether they are in such industries as retail trade or manufacturing, or in such occupational groupings as professional, technical, and so on.

The census also asks the *class* of worker: whether the person is employed as a local, state, or federal government employee; employed by a nonprofit or for-profit organization; self-employed (in an incorporated or nonincorporated business); or is working without pay in a family business or farm. The 1980 census "employee of private company" response was divided in 1990 between those working for profit-making companies or individuals, and those working for not-for-profit, tax-exempt, or charitable organizations. The questions on weeks worked in the year preceding the census were similar in 1980 and 1990, except that the 1980 question on how many weeks were spent on layoff and looking for a job was dropped.

INCOME AND POVERTY:
BETTER SPECIFICATION OF INCOME SOURCES

The income questions are also similar in 1980 and 1990, except that several sources were either added or specified more exactly (income from estates and trusts, and non-Social Security retirement, survivor, or disability pensions). This change will allow researchers to analyze 1990 *pension income* as a separate category for the first time (i.e., it is not commingled with other income sources). Given the ongoing debate over income distribution and entitlements among America's senior citizens, this change may allow researchers new insights into who is getting what, where, and why.

The Bureau of the Census generally computes income not as an individual characteristic, but rather as a characteristic of families, or more commonly of households. In these cases all of the income of the group (the family or household) is added together, and that sum is the new variable (family or household income).

Perhaps the most widely used and least understood statistics from the census are "poverty status" figures. These statistics are complex, because whether a family is in poverty is not just a simple measure of total family income or even of number of family members divided by total income. Instead, poverty status is affected by number of family members (in a nonlinear fashion), size of family income, age of children, and even age of the householder. Tables showing the "poverty thresholds" of family income for families of different composition in terms of 1989 income (as reported on the 1990 census form) can be found in the *Guide: Part A. Text* (U.S. Bureau of the Census, 1992e, p. 16) or in any state's *Summary Social, Economic and Housing Characteristics* (1990 CPH-5-15, U.S. Bureau of the Census [1992i], Appendix B, p. 28).

Due to inflation and some changes in the definition of poverty, the absolute levels of the poverty threshold of income have changed since 1980. The measure itself has remained roughly the same, however: It is the minimum level of acceptable subsistence income for a family or household (see Jencks, 1991; Levy, 1987).

DISABILITY STATUS: NEW RESEARCH OPPORTUNITIES

The 1980 census included a long-form question that asked whether each person had "a physical, mental or other health condition" that limited the amount or kind of work the person could do, prevented the person from working, or prevented the person from using public transportation. The 1990 long-form questionnaire retains the questions about health conditions that limit or prevent working at a job. A new question asks whether any person in the household has a health condition that limits his or her ability to go outside the home alone or causes difficulty in taking care of personal needs ("such as bathing, dressing, or getting around inside the home").

The 1990 census reflects the demands that an aging population will place on social service agencies. Although the impact of health conditions on employment are still of concern, the Bureau of the Census is also attempting to measure the kinds of social services that may be needed. Because this question has never been asked before on the census, creative researchers (especially those with an applied orientation) may link it to a variety of other areal and individual-level factors. A glance at the Illinois place-level data on this question (i.e., for both the under- and over-65 age groups) showed a surprising amount of variability between areas, suggesting that disability is concentrated heavily among certain population groups. These kinds of data have obvious implications for the efficient and equitable distribution of services for the disabled as well.

How Do Census Data Compare With Data From Other Sources?

The Bureau of the Census takes a number of repeated cross-sectional surveys, such as the Current Population Survey (CPS), as do private groups (the Gallup polls, for example), and nonprofit groups like the National Opinion Research Center (the General Social Survey). A census provides, in the most literal sense, a flood of data: It is a mile wide and only a foot deep. The census gives relatively superficial levels of measurement on a limited number of topics, but it captures every geographic area and even very small demographic groups that can be easily missed by 1,200-person (or even 200,000-person) national surveys.

For this reason, the census is highly prized by those who study local areas and by researchers who want to investigate relatively rare groups. National or even regionally based surveys never provide enough respondents to characterize either group. If your research question delves into either of these areas, you may want or have to use census data.

Census data often provide much more complete household or family data than does the average telephone survey. Such surveys might have to devote almost half of their time to obtaining even the short-form census roster of household members and their characteristics; because time is money in survey research, they usually content themselves with a much more cursory overview (number of household members, their age and sex, etc.) and concentrate solely on the individual respondent.

Researchers who are interested in household or family characteristics, or whose theories require detailed analysis of household rosters may find the census a superior source of data. For example, only census data may tell much about such questions as whether the secret of how many Asian American households can attain high rates of adult labor force participation is because of the frequent presence of elderly members who can contribute child care.

Census data are weaker than surveys in several key areas. First, census data ask no attitudinal questions. Because many theories of social action are vitally concerned with why persons behave the way they do, this means that the researcher has to supply the missing link of motivation in explaining census data without any evidence as to what the respondents actually thought.

Because censuses are done every 10 years and because the questions are not always the same, censuses are often weaker than surveys that are repeated at frequent intervals (such as the annual General Social Survey or the Current Population Surveys) in establishing when social trends began. These repeated cross-sectional surveys can also help to determine whether what appears to be a social trend from census to census may simply be an artifact of the different wording of a question.

In fact, a glance at several demography journals will show that national-level research on family demography, fertility, migration, and similar topics is actually much more dependent on the CPS or similar surveys than on the decennial census because more in-depth questions are used in the former instruments. The frequency of administration of these surveys also allows researchers to pinpoint when social trends begin and end with greater precision.

Over the past two or three decades, three large, national-level longitudinal surveys (i.e., panel surveys where the respondents are interviewed at specified intervals) have been developed. These include the National Longitudinal Survey at Ohio State University (the NLS; see Center for Human Resource Research, 1992), the University of Michigan's Panel Study of Income Dynamics (the PSID; see Hill, 1992), and the U.S. government's Survey of Income and Program Participation (SIPP; see Hunt, 1985, pp. 98-154). All three of these are high-quality sources of social and economic data on households and individuals.

If a research question revolves around the changing fortunes of people, on the causal ordering of events at the individual level, or on the hazards or contingencies of the occurrence of certain events (does a wife working more make a husband work less, or vice versa?), then these data sets will be far more satisfactory than census data, which have only very limited time depth or horizons built into their questions. On the other hand, learning how to use and obtain useful data from these longitudinal data sets is a major proposition in terms of the commitment of time, energy, and computing resources.

In summary: There are probably more topics that can be analyzed using 1980 and 1990 census data than for any prior pair of censuses. Data in electronic media from both censuses should encourage research on social change, and the TIGER mapping technology should lead to enhanced use of graphic representation of data.

The key problem in comparing 1980 and 1990 census data will be the education question. Census data remain superior to survey data in finding rare populations and in examining local areas. Some researchers may find using 1990 census data leads to further research requiring the use of cross-sectional or longitudinal (with their greater time depth) surveys to complete the analysis.

2. Design of the 1990 Census

Key Concepts in Using Census Data

The design of the 1990 census must be of concern to researchers because it places significant limits on the kinds of research that can be done and ways in which this research can be undertaken.

There are three key areas of misunderstanding about the census:

a. the long versus the short form of the census
b. the Bureau of the Census's systems of geography and how they affect the availability of data
c. where to look for census data

A lack of understanding of these concepts is likely to lead to a lack of understanding of what kinds of census data can be used for hypothesis-testing, how they can be used, and how to obtain them.

DATA FROM THE COMPLETE COUNT
VERSUS DATA FROM THE SAMPLE COUNT

As in 1980, there were two kinds of census questionnaires distributed to U.S. households in 1990:

a. the "short form," which was filled out by all households (a 100% sample)

b. the "long form," a census form that contained *all* the short-form questions *and* many other questions

The short form asked seven population questions of every person and seven questions about the household's housing conditions. The long form included *all* of the short-form questions, 26 more questions about each person in the household, and 19 more household housing questions.

About 106 million housing units received the short form, and 17.7 million housing units received the long form. The *long form* was not randomly distributed across the United States. A far higher proportion of households in smaller, less populous areas received it. For example, households in counties and incorporated places with populations of less than 2,500 persons in 1988 were sampled at a rate of 1 in 2. Places with populations above 2,500 received one long form for every six households, and some densely populated census tracts and block numbering areas received one long form for every eight households.

The Bureau of the Census samples areas at different rates because of the different needs of various populations. Many population characteristics are estimated from the census samples of the long form, and these estimates are used for a variety of planning purposes. If the 1-in-6 sampling ratio were used in many rural areas, the degree of sampling uncertainty (i.e., the width of the confidence interval) would be so great that these estimates would be almost unusable (see Chapter 3).

The Bureau of the Census takes advantage of the fact that areas with large populations (such as census tracts or blocks in urban areas) have such large populations that a 1-in-6 or 1-in-8 sampling ratio can be used with relatively little increase in the confidence interval. There is also another, more practical reason why a 1-in-2 sampling ratio is used in rural areas: Mistakes in location of facilities for the population (roads, power lines, etc.) are often far more expensive if the population is widely dispersed.

EFFECTS OF CENSUS DESIGN ON RESEARCH

Census questions thought to be essential to an accurate description of the population down to the lowest levels of aggregation (i.e., down to the block or block-group level) are included in the 100% component. In 1990, these questions included age, sex, marital status, value of home, and so on.

30

Topics that are of less local importance are asked in the sample component. These questions include a much broader range of topics, including some questions that sometimes will only apply to a small part of the population, such as the questions on functional disability or veteran status.

It is important to know whether a topic is on the 100% or sample component because this has major implications for

a. how low a geographic level of aggregation one can find the topic (one can find population by race down to the block level, but not population by veteran status)
b. whether the topic can be cross-classified by other topics (race and sex can be cross-classified down to the block level, but not fertility and race)
c. on what media (printed volumes, computer tapes, CD-ROMs, etc.) the data can be found

Census Geography

The Bureau of the Census produces data in a variety of geographic formats. A very brief introduction to the major systems of the geographic hierarchy will be given here. Because it is difficult to understand the geography of either printed or electronic census data without a knowledge of how these areal units are related, this topic deserves close study. A good introduction to Bureau of the Census geography and geographical products can be found in *Maps and More* (U.S. Bureau of the Census, 1992d).

The Bureau of the Census has divided the United States into a complete and exhaustive set of areal units for use in the compilation of census data. Census areas are generally *hierarchical:* Each smaller unit usually fits entirely within the next larger one in the hierarchy.

There are several major hierarchies. The standard 1990 Bureau of the Census schematic diagram of how these units fit together is given in Chart 2.1. This hierarchy is somewhat different from the one used in 1980.

Starting from the top of Chart 2.1, the United States is divided into four statistical regions. These regions are split among nine divisions, each of which is made up of varying numbers of states.

Within states there are two separate hierarchies, "Places" and counties. "Places" can exist outside of or overlap county boundaries;

31

THE 1990 CENSUS OF POPULATION AND HOUSING

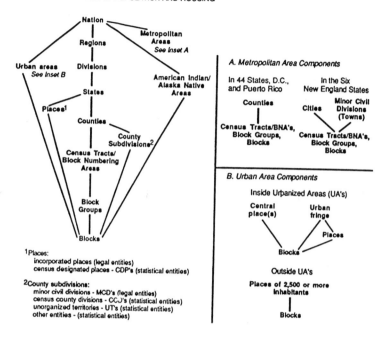

Chart 2.1. Geographic Hierarchy of Administrative and Statistical Units Used in the 1990 Census
SOURCE: U.S. Bureau of the Census, 1993a, p. 20.

for example, the city of Elgin, Illinois (an incorporated place), had 15,400 of its population in Cook County and 77,010 in Kane County in 1990.

Below the county level there are two separate hierarchies: county subdivisions (which can be either statistical or legal entities) and census tracts/block numbering areas (which are statistical entities). Usually, counties in urban areas are divided into census tracts and those in nonurban areas are divided into block numbering areas (which are collections of contiguous block groups), but there are a few exceptions to this rule.

Below the census tract/block numbering level there are block groups—collections of contiguous blocks. The lowest level of areal data collection is the block. In the 1990 census, "blocks" are found in

CHART 2.2. Number of Major Geographic Entities in the 1990 Census

	Number
1. Legal or administrative entities	
State	50
District of Columbia	1
Outlying areas (Guam, Puerto Rico, etc.)	6
Counties and equivalent entities	3,248
Minor Civil Divisions (MCDs)	30,386
Incorporated places	19,365
Congressional districts	435
ZIP codes	29,469
2. Statistical entities	
Regions	4
Divisions	9
Metropolitan Statistical Areas (MSAs)	268
Consolidated MSAs (CMSAs)	21
Primary MSAs (PMSAs)	73
Census Designated Places (CDPs)	4,423
Census tracts	50,690
Block Numbering Areas (BNAs)	11,586
Block Groups (BGs)	229,192
Blocks	7,017,425

SOURCE: U.S. Bureau of the Census, 1992a.

both urban and rural areas, so they sometimes can have widely divergent sizes, shapes, and population sizes.

The 1990 census designations of urban and metropolitan areas are too complex to be treated here (see Marx, 1990; U.S. Bureau of the Census, 1992d, 1993a). One major change between 1980 and 1990 is a terminological one: 1980's Standard Metropolitan Statistical Areas (SMSAs) are now called Metropolitan Statistical Areas (MSAs). A new designation of *large city* (the Primary MSA, or PMSA) has been added below the *megalopolis* (the Consolidated MSA) level. For some reason these units (which will be widely used by social scientists) are not named in either insets A or B (Metropolitan Area Components or Urban Area Components) of the official Bureau of the Census chart reproduced as Chart 2.1.

One key decision faced by those planning to do research using ecological units from the 1990 census will be what unit or units to choose. Chart 2.2 shows the number of units (nationwide) for selected levels of these hierarchies (not all levels are mentioned here). A state-level breakdown of these units can also be found (see U.S. Bureau of the Census, 1993a).

For many national- or regional-level analyses, counties may be a good choice as units of analysis. There are about 3,200 counties (3,141 within the United States proper), and much additional descriptive data on counties can be obtained from the U.S. Bureau of the Census's *County and City Databook*. For other regional analyses or comparisons, the MSA, PMSA/MSA, or CMSA/MSA levels of analysis may be more useful, particularly if there is a reason to consider an entire urban area as a unit of analysis.

For local analysis the census tract or even the block group may be an adequate operationalization of a "local area." For some cities, such as Chicago, social scientists have constructed neighborhoods out of census tracts (see Chicago Fact Book Consortium, 1984). In Chicago many city agencies and social scientists produce neighborhood data for different parts of the city. Of course, they are using neighborhood boundaries that existed more than 50 years ago (before the large-scale Black and Hispanic migrations, before the major highways were built, and so on), but they are consistent over time.

One problem with using census tract data to follow time-series trends through different censuses is that apparently the Bureau of the Census will not be publishing any guides to how census tract boundaries have changed between 1980 and 1990. As a result, any attempt to match census tract data between 1980 (or earlier censuses) and 1990 may require considerable time and effort. In urban areas that were largely built up by the time of earlier censuses, this is not a major problem; the tract numbers are probably largely the same. Yet in some cities—such as Sun Belt ones—the rapid inclusion of formerly rural territory may create problems for researchers attempting to match equivalent tract numbers in succeeding censuses. Here is one case where getting in touch with the appropriate census State Data Center (their addresses and telephone numbers are given in the annual *Census Catalog and Guide)* or a local planning agency may help a great deal.

Data Products: Choices and Constraints

After the researcher has decided on what census questions to use and the units of analysis, it is necessary to choose between different sources of census data. Because the same data are frequently available in several media, the choice of data source is dependent on (a) the size of the data set that will be created, (b) the researcher's hardware and software resources, and (c) the kinds of demands (in terms of data modification, analysis, and recall capabilities) that will be placed on the data set.

DATA AVAILABLE IN PRINTED FORM

The Bureau of the Census publishes statistics on every locality in the United States. Not all of these may be of interest, however; the general rule is: The smaller the area, the fewer the available published cross-tabulations.

There are three major series of printed reports:

a. the CPH (Census of Population and Housing) series: These reports include information on *both* population and housing characteristics. Within this series, three reports (CPH-1, CPH-2, and CPH-6) are based solely on 100% enumeration data, one (CPH-5) is based only on sample (long-form) data, and two reports (CPH-3 and CPH-4) are based on 100% and sample data.

b. the CP (Census of Population) series: These reports include only population data. Within this series, the CP-1 reports are based only on 100% data, whereas the CP-2 reports are based on sample data. Several of these printed reports give totals for the entire U.S. population, not state totals.

c. the CH (Census of Housing) series: These reports only cover housing data. In this series, the CH-1 reports are based on 100% data, and the CH-2 reports are based on sample data. A number of these reports are also at the national rather than state level (U.S. Bureau of the Census, 1992e, pp. 76-79).

Chart 2.3 (adapted from U.S. Bureau of the Census, 1992e, p. 81) shows which of the six CPH, two CP, and two CH series reports cover various geographic areas. Coverage (as marked by an "X") means only that one or more tables in the report covers this level of aggregation in any particular state or territory. This table's value is chiefly exclusive: It tells which reports (or series of reports) will not cover a certain level of geography, and which ones might be of some use. Every state, the District of Columbia, Puerto Rico, and the U.S. Virgin Islands has a printed volume in the CPH-1, CPH-2, CPH-5, CP-1, CP-2, CH-1, and CH-2 report series (see Chart 2.3, and U.S. Bureau of the Census, 1992e, pp. 76-79, for more details and 1980 census equivalent publication data).

CHART 2.3. Geographic Areas Covered in Printed 1990 Census Reports

	1	2	1990 CPH 3	4	5	1990 CP 1	2	1990 CH 1	2
United States, regions, divisions	X	X	—	—	X	X	X	X	X
States and statistical equivalents	X	X	—	X	X	X	X	X	X
Metropolitan areas	X	X	X	—	X	X	X	X	X
Urbanized areas	X	X	—	—	X	X	X	X	X
Counties and statistical equivalents	X	X	X	X	X	X	X	X	X
American Indian and Alaska Native areas	X	—	—	X	X	X	X	X	X
Congressional districts	—	—	—	X	—	—	—	—	—
Places (by population size)									
Under 1,000	X	X	—	—	X	—	—	—	—
1,000 and over	X	X	—	—	X	X	—	X	—
2,500 and over	X	X	—	—	X	X	X	X	X
10,000 and over	X	X	X	X	X	X	X	X	X
County subdivisions (by type)									
MCDs in 12 states	X	X	—	X	X	X	X	X	X
MCDs in 8 states	X	X	—	—	X	X	—	X	—
Subdivisions in other states and statistical equivalents	X	X	—	—	X	X	—	X	—
County subdivisions (by population size) MCDs									
Under 1,000	X	X	—	—	X	X	—	X	—
1,000 and over	X	X	—	—	X	X	—	X	—
2,500 and over	X	X	—	—	X	X	X	X	X
10,000 and over	X	X	—	X	X	X	X	X	X
CCDs	X	X	—	—	X	X	—	X	—
Census tracts/BNAs	—	—	X	—	—	—	—	—	—

SOURCE: U.S. Bureau of the Census, 1992e, pp. 76-81.
NOTE: 1990 CPH-6 Report only covers nonstate areas (Guam, Palau, etc.).

There are also several series of reports issued for selected areas or for the United States as a whole that provide information on various topics. For example, *CP-1-1C, General Population Characteristics for Urbanized Areas,* gives detailed statistics on age, sex, race, and so on

36

(100% sample) for individual UAs (Urbanized Areas). For UAs split by state boundaries, it provides information on the UA as a whole and on the subtotals for the part of the UA in each separate state.

Four census publications for each state (and for the District of Columbia, Puerto Rico, and the U.S. Virgin Islands) will be of most use to researchers in the preliminary stage of an investigation:

CP-1. General Population Characteristics. This volume is based on the 100% sample (i.e., the short form) and gives cross-tabulated statistics on race, Hispanic origin, age, marital status, and so forth for states, counties, places, or county subdivisions. This is the basic reference volume for the general population characteristics of the local areas of any state or territory.

CPH-5. Summary Social, Economic, and Housing Characteristics. This volume is based on sample data (i.e., from the long form) and gives cross-tabulated statistics on a variety of subjects for states, counties, places, and subcounty divisions. These tables often provide much more refined data than can be found in the *CP-1. General Population Characteristics* because they cover data from the sample questions. Of course, because the data are derived from samples (which usually range from about 10% to 50% of the total population), these data are subject to sampling variability.

CH-1. General Housing Characteristics. This report summarizes statistics on unit value or rent, number of rooms, tenure, vacancy characteristics, and so on for states, counties, places, and subcounty divisions. It is based on the 100% sample (the short form).

CH-2. Detailed Housing Characteristics. Based on the sample questions on housing (long form), this report includes more extensive tabular data (broken down by more population groups) than the previous report. It covers states, counties, places, and subcounty divisions.

Anyone interested in the analysis of a locality would be well advised to buy at least the population (CP-1) and population and housing (CPH-5) volumes for that state, and perhaps the housing volumes (CH-1 and CH-2) as well. These reports will be a constant source of data for denominators for rates and comparative data on surrounding or similar localities. They are also very good guides to how data are structured on the Summary Tape File (STF) tapes or CD-ROMs, and how the tables generated from STF tapes or other census tape sources should look.

Close study of the tables in these volumes (i.e., adding and subtracting rows and columns in puzzling tables until they finally make sense) can give a novice researcher a window into the organizational mind, logic, and traditions of the Bureau of the Census. Although there is nothing particularly mysterious about the organization of census data, researchers often find it confusing at first.

FINDING THE RIGHT INFORMATION
IN PRINTED CENSUS TABLES

Researchers undertaking ecological data analysis often face a key question: Do the data I need exist for the unit (or level of aggregation) for which I need them?

The census makes the search for the answer easier by providing a "Table Finding Guide" at the beginning of each tabular volume of the 1990 census. In the 1980 census volumes, the Table Finding Guide was conveniently located on the inside front cover; in the 1990 volumes the Guide can be found at the beginning of Section II in each volume.

The Table Finding Guide theoretically enables the reader to discover at what level of aggregation a subject is treated. Once the needed geographic level is determined, the table number can be found in the appropriate cell of the Guide. Because the same tables are available for every state in published volumes, it is usually only necessary to consult one Table Finding Guide to discover at what level of aggregation variables exist, even if the data will come from a number of states.

The Table Finding Guide classifies subject matter by geographic level and may show whether the table gives racial or Hispanic origin subtotals as well. For example, suppose a researcher is interested in age distributions in rural areas. The Table Finding Guide for *CPH-1, General Population Characteristics*, shows that age by single year is only available at the state level. Age by 5-year intervals (and by single years up to age 22) is available for the urban and rural region of the state by race. If, however, the researcher wants to obtain age in the rural areas of particular counties, then only 5-year age group data are available, and they do not include racial or Hispanic origin totals. The systematic use of the Table Finding Guide can save a researcher hours of flipping through printed tables to see if independent and dependent variables can be matched up at the same areal levels.

Even though the Table Finding Guide is useful, it is usually a good idea to look up the table to be sure that what should be in a table is really there. The other reason one should actually look up the table is that the Guide is not always clear about how two or more variables are cross-classified in a table. For example, suppose a researcher is interested in how Hispanic householders were distributed by race in Illinois in 1990. From the Table Finding Guide (p. II-1) of the *CPH-1-15, Summary of Population and Housing Characteristics, Illinois* (U.S. Bureau of the Census, 1992i), we learn that state-level (and data for different sub-state categories) totals by "race of householder" are available in that volume's Table 13.

Looking up this table in that volume's "List of Statistical Tables," we find that Table 13's complete title is "Occupied Housing Units by Race and Hispanic Origin of Householder, 1990; by State, County, County Subdivision and Place." From the Table Finding Guide it appeared Table 13 would only give race of householder, not householders by Hispanic origin status. Yet the conjunction "and" in the title of Table 13 seems to promise that race should be cross-classified by Hispanic origin status somewhere in this table on householders. In reality, neither is quite true.

From Table 13 it is possible to find out the number of householders who are of Hispanic origin by race. Yet it is not given directly; it must be computed.

One part of Table 13 lists "race of householder" and the totals for householders of each race (without any information on Hispanic origin). Another subsection lists the numbers of "householders not of Hispanic origin" by race. By subtracting the latter category from the former one, it is possible to compute the number of householders of each race who are of Hispanic origin, even though these categories are not given in any part of the table.

Obviously, it can be dangerous to take the Table Finding Guide or the List of Statistical Tables too literally. It is frequently advisable to work through a few examples of the data that are sought from printed or electronic media before deciding whether or not the data exist in an appropriate form for an area.

GEOGRAPHIC DATA PRODUCTS
AVAILABLE ON COMPUTER TAPE

Any information available in printed form for the 1990 census is also available on computer tape. In fact, due to the cost of printing census volumes, many more data are available on computer tape than in printed form.

The key steps in using computer tapes are to (a) identify the variables or raw data of interest from the census; (b) identify how the variable is coded on the computer tape (how wide are the age or housing value data groupings, for example); (c) identify whether the data are available for the desired geographic unit; and (d) read the census data from the computer tape to a statistical analysis package with the appropriate specifications of variable labels and designations of geographic units. If this is done correctly then the census data can be used directly or transformed (within the statistical package) in different ways to suit the researcher's theoretical purposes.

The Bureau of the Census does not provide data on magnetic tape that can be input directly into programs like SPSS or SAS. Most users will need some guidance because the way in which hierarchical geographic census files are organized makes the job fairly complex, and computer programmers are not usually familiar with Bureau of the Census data conventions. This task is not a very difficult one for an experienced programmer, however. Dowell Myers (1992, pp. 343-347) has included simple programs for transferring STF (Summary Tape Files, the computer files of geographically based data) and PUMS files from their original format to a SAS input program in his monograph.

Fortunately, the Inter-university Consortium for Political and Social Research (ICPSR) at the University of Michigan's Institute for Social Research has acquired all of the major census tapes for 1990. It will provide them to researchers at its 370 member institutions together with programs written in SPSS and SAS that will allow the original data to be easily transferred into case-variable format. The ICPSR will provide its members all of the census tapes mentioned in this chapter; current availability status can be found by consulting the annual ICPSR catalog or recent issues of the *ICPSR Bulletin*. The ICPSR plans to concentrate on making statistical data from the census available, not on providing geographic information products such as TIGER files.

An excellent introduction to census computer tape products can be found in the 1990 *CPH-R-1A Guide. Part A. Text* (U.S. Bureau of the Census, 1992e, pp. 82-92), and technical documentation can be found in such guides as *Summary Tape File 1. Technical Documentation* (U.S. Bureau of the Census, 1991). Figure 5.5 in the *Guide* (U.S. Bureau of the Census, 1992e, pp. 84-85) shows the kinds of data found in each of the four Summary Tape Files (STFs), and how these STFs are divided into subcategories that constitute the actual magnetic tapes themselves.

The STF-1 and STF-2 tapes include different data, but both are from the short form (100% sample) of the census. The letter designations (STF-1A, STF-2C, and so on) denote different geographic hierarchies for the data. Congressional district data can be found on STF-1D, whereas STF-1 data at the block level can only be found on the STF-1B tape. The STF-3 and STF-4 tape sets contain data from the sample (long-form) population and housing characteristics. Generally, one STF tape holds the data on one state (although large states may require more than one tape), and they are ordered on a state-by-state basis. These tapes are provided on 9-track reels, formatted as either 6,250 or 1,600 bytes per inch, labeled or unlabeled, in either EBCDIC or ASCII formats. The same data can be ordered on tape cartridges compatible with IBM 3480 systems (or with DEC VAX TA90 or Storage Tek 4780 tape subsystems). The data on these tapes are basically arranged in a rectangular form (by level of geography). However, the repetition of geographic cell totals by race and Hispanic origin totals in the STF-2 and STF-4 tapes means that they can also be thought of as "semi-hierarchical" files, and treated accordingly when the files are read into a statistical package (Erik Austin, personal communication, May 5, 1993).

One interesting feature of the STF computer files is the inclusion of the number of persons and housing units allocated or substituted (see Chapter 3) in any geographic unit. Thus, unlike the printed volumes, it is possible to see how many and what kinds of persons in local areas had imputed values, and what aspects of housing (vacancy status, value, etc.) were imputed as well.

PUBLIC USE MICRODATA SAMPLE (PUMS) COMPUTER TAPES

The PUMS files are actually two separate computer files:

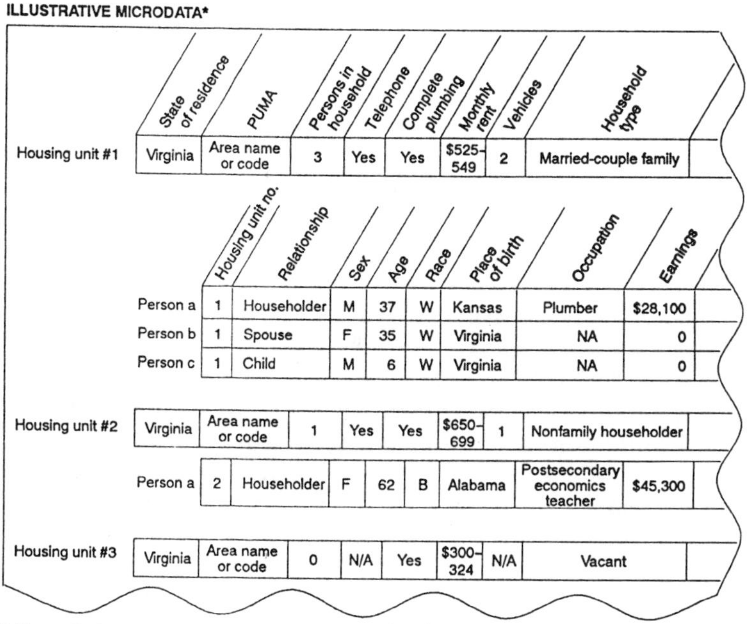

ILLUSTRATIVE MICRODATA*

* Public-use microdata samples do not actually contain alphabetic information. Such information is converted to numeric codes; for example, the State of Virginia has a numeric code of 51.

Chart 2.4. Structure of Household and Individual Data on Public Use Microdata Sample (PUMS) Magnetic Tape File
SOURCE: U.S. Bureau of the Census, 1992e, p. 90.

a. the 5% sample (each household with long-form data), organized by counties or county groups of at least 100,000 persons (these units do not cross state boundaries)

b. the 1% sample (also of households with long-form data), organized by metropolitan areas or similar large areas that may cross state boundaries

The PUMS tapes are more complex to use because the data are organized *hierarchically*; that is, the data on individual household members are attached to data on their housing unit, family type, and so on (see Chart 2.4).

Fortunately, many statistical software packages such as SPSS, BMDP, and SAS can recognize and deal with these hierarchical data formats (U.S. Bureau of the Census, 1992e, p. 91). As a result, putting very large PUMS data files into these software systems is a much easier job.

Of course, some attention must still be paid to whether census data dictionaries and data transforms can be read by any particular statistical package or require some modification. Researchers at ICPSR member institutions will be able to get both the 1% and the 5% PUMS in SPSS or SAS file formats, which should make data entry much easier.

Researchers who use the 5% PUMS will have access to more than 5 million housing units and 12 million persons (Campbell, 1993, p. 2). Most users will want to focus either on a much more defined area (the PUMS for suburban Philadelphia, perhaps) or on a restricted national-level population (all migrants from Greece born before 1950 in the PUMS, for example) to reduce the sample size to a size manageable by a workstation or personal computer.

If a national sample is needed it is possible to reduce the sample proportion from the original 5 per 100 to perhaps 1 per 1,000 with little increase in sampling error and great gains in computing speed and ease of storage and retrieval. The Bureau of the Census can provide guidance on how a properly designed and weighted extract of PUMS data can be constructed (Campbell, 1993, p. 2).

OTHER 1990 CENSUS COMPUTER FILES

There are three other summary files besides the Summary Tape Files and the PUMS files that may be of use to many researchers:

1. *1990 Census/Equal Opportunity File.* This file tabulates educational attainment and detailed occupations by age for different major racial groups and for the Hispanic-origin population. It is available for places with at least 50,000 persons, metropolitan areas, counties, and states. This file will be a major source of data for those interested in patterns of social stratification, labor market activity, and similar topics.

2. *County-to-County Migration File.* As the name suggests, this file cross-classifies the answers to long-form Question 14 (Where did you live five years ago?) by past and current county of residence. It also includes descriptive information on the characteristics of persons in these migration streams.

3. *Population and Housing Counts File.* This file (released in early 1991) gives total counts for both individuals and housing units for geographic regions down to places (as well as for American Indian and

Alaska Native areas). Most of the relatively simple information on this tape has been superseded by the data released on STF-1, STF-3, and other tapes released in 1992 and 1993.

The first of these data sets is available on tape, CD-ROM, and microfiche; the second on tape and CD-ROM; and the third only on tape (U.S. Bureau of the Census, 1992e, p. 89).

These descriptions of census computer tapes should not give the novice user the idea that plunging into census data will be free of frustration, dead ends, illogical formats, and so on. In fact, it is somewhat surprising how little attention the Bureau of the Census pays to showing how its large-scale products can be used with different commercial software products.

It is also surprising that only a few technical specialists at the larger software firms know how to enter census data correctly into their firm's product. Apparently most statistical software firms see the census data user market as too small or too dispersed to tailor a specific product for 1990 census data entry to them. The last such product was written by researchers at SPSS in 1984 for use with the 1980 census tapes, and my research indicates that none of the big firms have any similar project on the drawing board for the 1990 census. As a result, researchers who are not associated with institutions with ICPSR membership may be highly dependent on informal networks of users at their own institutions, at census-designated State Data Centers, or within their own professional organizations to learn how to move raw census data from tapes to commercial software products.

DATA AVAILABLE ON MICROFICHE

All of the printed volumes of the 1990 census are also available on microfiche. In addition, the Bureau of the Census has taken a great deal of local area data from the Summary Tape Files (STFs) that are not available in printed volumes (i.e., at the block and block group level) and made them available on microfiche. Each piece of microfiche holds the equivalent of about 208 pages of printed text (U.S. Bureau of the Census, 1992e, p. 92).

Depending on the subject matter, microfiche is sold for both counties and states. Researchers who need to make frequent reference to local area data in a relatively random way, or who do not have the computer resources (or technical expertise) to support the purchase

44

of census tapes may find that microfiche suits their purposes. Of course, if a researcher plans to build a complete statistical data set for an area the transfer of data from computer tape or from CD-ROM sources is much more efficient than taking it from microfiche.

DATA AVAILABLE ON CD-ROM

Another key technical breakthrough of the 1990 census is the provision of a large amount of census data (including files equivalent to the state-level STF and PUMS computer tapes) in CD-ROM form. The provision of census data on CD-ROMs means that anyone with a personal computer and a CD-ROM reader can now gain access to electronic census data. Such access previously required a much more expensive magnetic tape reader.

CD-ROMs can hold vast amounts of data; the Bureau of the Census packs up to 650 megabytes of data on its CDs. They can be run on almost any IBM or clone personal computer with MS-DOS 3.1 or higher and a DOS file manager with CD-ROM extension capability (see U.S. Bureau of the Census, [n. d.], p. J-1). Some CD-ROM readers, however, can take a long time to transfer large amounts of data to the hard drive of a personal computer.

CD-ROMs from the Bureau of the Census come with built-in (GO) software, which allows the user to download the data in one of three forms: (a) in tabular form (which is how it appears on the computer screen); (b) in dBase III+ form (an input format recognized by several spreadsheet and data analysis programs); and (c) as an ASCII case-variable file, suitable for input into most statistical analysis programs.

The early versions of this GO software would only perform the first task. The Bureau of the Census has fixed this problem, and version 2.1 of the GO program works correctly. Users who have the old version of the GO software can call the Bureau of the Census's electronic bulletin board at (301) 763-7554 and download the corrected program (Ken Taylor, personal communication, August 5, 1993).

MERGING GEOGRAPHIC AND STATISTICAL DATA FOR ANALYSIS

One of the most exciting possibilities to emerge from the 1990 census is the ability to use geographic TIGER files (see Chapter 1) and census data to map the distribution of different variables. There are several programs now on the market that can be used to process TIGER files and build maps that are usable with personal computers. They include MapInfo, ArcInfo, Atlas, SASGraph, and GeoSight Factfinder.

In general, these Geographic Information Systems (GIS) link their geographic area files to something akin to a spreadsheet of data (in several cases it actually is a commercially available spreadsheet), and then draw maps (in different colors, cross-hatching, etc.) of the variables desired. These maps can typically be displayed on a video terminal or printed out.

These systems usually have a relatively low level of statistical sophistication. For example, most statistical tasks, such as mapping the areal residuals of a regression equation, must be done in conjunction with a statistical package like SPSS or SAS.

These systems are evolving rapidly. The past few years have seen such a rapid decline in price of computer memory (of which these GIS demand a lot) that many researchers may want to look into purchasing them. There has also been progress in the area of refining and decreasing the size of TIGER files, another technical problem too lengthy to discuss here.

3. Procedures and Problems of the 1990 Census

In the previous chapter a brief description was given of the kinds of data available to the researcher from the 1990 census. Yet any serious researcher must have some understanding of how these data were obtained from the population. This chapter will give an introduction to 1990 census procedures and to the problems encountered in the Bureau's nationwide enumeration process. The Post-Enumeration Survey (PES), a large-scale survey conducted in conjunction with the census that provides important information on the number and characteristics of undercounted and erroneously enumerated persons, will be described. Census policies and procedures on data presentation and the preservation of confidentiality and their implications for research will be introduced.

Preparations for the 1990 Census

The Bureau of the Census had to compile an address list of more than 100 million housing units in order to conduct the 1990 census. From the 1980 census the Bureau already had maps and address lists of all housing units at that time. Yet a large number of housing units had been demolished, moved, divided, built, or otherwise changed since 1980.

To ensure adequate coverage of all household units the Bureau of the Census purchased more than 50 million addresses of households in metropolitan areas from commercial sources. These name and address lists were updated and checked by census workers, postal employees, and local government officials and were combined with preexisting lists used for the 1980 census to form the source for the initial wave of the 1990 mail-out of census forms.

Chart 3.1 gives a schematic outline of the proportions of the population covered by the three major methods used to enumerate housing units throughout the United States and a rough outline of the procedures used in each method.

The Bureau of the Census relied primarily on mail-out, mail-back census forms. This process was much cheaper than door-to-door interviewing. Throughout the country, census forms were mailed out on March 23, 1990, with instructions for household members to complete the forms and mail them back by April 1.

When a housing unit did not send back a census questionnaire, the Bureau of the Census had to send out workers (often on multiple trips) to find its location and determine if it was a residential structure. If so, enumerators had to find out if it was occupied. Because the 1990 census was also a census of housing, vacant and occupied units were counted. Finally, if it was known to be occupied, the enumerator had to find someone there willing to fill out the census form, which could involve multiple visits. About 34.4 million households were enumerated by 157,000 Bureau of the Census employees.

When enumerators could not contact even one inhabitant of a dwelling unit after numerous tries, they were permitted to obtain "last resort" information from someone else in the neighborhood,

CHART 3.1. Methods Used to Enumerate U.S. Housing Units in 1990

I. **Housing units enumerated through Mailout-Mailback Technique**
(84% of all housing units)
   A. Units enumerated through the use of mailing lists (63% of all
      mailout-mailback housing units)
      1. Original mailing lists (from commercial and other sources) provide
         51.6 million addresses (1988).
      2. Advanced Post Office Check (APOC), 1988-1989: letter carriers given
         mailing lists; they add 1.6 million addresses.
      3. Census workers precanvass (Summer, 1989): workers visit all areas
         on mailing lists, view housing structures from the outside, add 6
         million housing units.
      4. Precensus local review (late 1989-early 1990): local government
         officials check census housing unit counts. Census workers
         recanvass blocks with large undercounts.
      5. Casing check (March 1990): addresses rechecked by postal workers
         before census forms were sent out.
   B. Units enumerated not using mailing lists (largely in rural and suburban
      areas, 37% of all mailout-mailback housing units)
      1. Prelist operation (June 1988-January 1989): all housing units in a
         locality listed by Bureau of the Census workers; 28 million housing
         units found.
      2. Postal check: census listings given to postal workers who add or
         change addresses.
      3. Census check: census field-workers verify Postal Service corrections
         of Bureau of the Census lists. Steps 2 and 3 add 1.2 million more
         housing unit addresses.

II. **Housing units enumerated using Update/Leave Procedure**
(10% of all housing units)
      1. Prelist operation: all housing units in area listed by Bureau of the
         Census workers. This technique used mainly in rural areas and in
         urban public housing projects.
      2. Census questionnaire dropped off by enumerator, then mailed back.

III. **Housing units enumerated by the List/Enumerate Procedure**
(6% of all housing units)
      1. Postal Service delivers census questionnaires in sparsely settled
         rural areas.
      2. Census enumerator picks up questionnaires and makes address lists
         as they are picked up.

---

such as a landlord or neighbor. Last resort information had to include
the number of persons resident there and information on at least three

of four key individual variables (sex, race, marital status, and relationship to the householder). Two key housing questions (owned or rented, and type of unit—i.e., house, apartment, trailer, etc.) for the unit also had to be ascertained.

Throughout the United States about 13.8% of all housing units enumerated during the Nonresponse Followup stage of the census (i.e., that part of the census where enumerators visited housing units that had failed to send back their questionnaires) were last resort cases. Again, this differed greatly by locale: Last resort cases constituted 19.9% of all housing units visited during this stage in Bureau of the Census Type 1 offices (in large central cities), 12.3% in Type 2 offices (rural areas, suburbs, and small cities), and 10.7% in Type 3 offices (low-density rural areas; see Eriksen et al., 1991, Appendix A, p. 74).

When a local Bureau of the Census office obtained returned questionnaires for at least 95% of its housing units, enumerators could go to the next stage: obtaining *closeout* data on housing units. Closeout data were more vague than last resort information: They included the kind of structure in which the unit was housed, the number of persons living there (or their names), and whether the unit was occupied. Persons living in urban areas, areas with high population turnover, and large proportions of minority inhabitants were more likely to be enumerated through closeout procedures.

In cases where a housing unit was known to exist and thought to be occupied, but where it was not possible by any means to discover how many persons lived there, the inhabitants were called "non-data defined" and reported as such. All of their characteristics were estimated through the *substitution* of data from nearby housing units, just as *imputation* was used to estimate the missing characteristics of households and individuals covered by the last resort and closeout procedures (see below).

Nationwide, census data for about 4.6 million people were collected through the last resort procedure, for 1.93 million people through the closeout procedure, and for 1.96 million people through the non–data-defined procedure (Eriksen et al., 1991, Appendix A, p. 27).

These categories constitute 1.86%, 0.78%, and 0.79% of the total enumerated population (247.8 million), respectively.

The Bureau of the Census also tried a variety of experimental follow-up techniques after the April 1990 original enumeration to improve coverage among underenumerated or special population groups. These programs included the vacancy-delete operation, the "Were

You Counted?" program, the housing coverage check, and the parolee/ probationer check. Although these methods did add some persons and housing units to the original count, there is evidence that the data obtained had very high rates of error (Eriksen et al., 1991, pp. 4-9).

Problems in Taking the 1990 Census

Two related problems of the 1990 census attracted considerable media attention: the low rate of mail-back of census forms and how long the census took in many areas. It was hoped that at least 70 million household forms would be returned by April 15, 1990. Instead, participation lagged, and the mail-back response rate was particularly low in many large cities.

In 1980, the national mail-back response rate for the census was about 75%. The Bureau of the Census projected a mail-back response rate of about 70% for 1990. Yet by April 25 only 65% of the mailed census forms were returned; in urban areas, the rate was 60% (compared to 66% in suburban and 64% in rural areas; see Eriksen et al., 1991, Appendix A, p. 17).

The low mail-back rate contributed to the increasing *cost* of the census. The Bureau of the Census had to hire and train many more enumerators. Because it turned out to be far harder to find householders than expected, there were delays and decreases in productivity (U.S. General Accounting Office, 1992, p. 45). The price of counting each housing unit grew from 11 dollars in 1970 to 20 dollars in 1980 and to 25 dollars in 1990 (each measured in 1990 dollars). The direct cost of administering the census shows only part of the picture, however. The total costs attributable to the 1990 census rose from 1.67 billion dollars for the 1980 census to 2.6 billion dollars for the 1990 census, a 65% increase (both in 1990 dollars; U.S. General Accounting Office, 1992, pp. 23-25).

Why was the response rate so low? Many households simply did not receive the forms in the mail. Follow-up face-to-face interviews by National Opinion Research Center interviewers indicated that, nationwide, about 8.5% of those who lived in a house, 16.6% of those who lived in a 2- to 4-apartment structure, 10.8% of those who lived in a structure with five or more apartments, and 10% of those who lived in a trailer said that their unit never received a census form through the mail at that time (Eriksen et al., 1991, p. 63).

The reasons why respondents never received their mailed (or in some cases, dropped-off) questionnaires are many and varied: poor quality of address lists, poor coordination between the U.S. Postal Service and the Bureau of the Census, unreported new construction, new housing units constructed within existing structures, census forms left in apartment house lobbies because they lacked apartment numbers, and so on. The Postal Service returned about 4.5 million census forms as undeliverable; in many cases, this was because the housing unit received its mail through a postal box number rather than through a street address (Eriksen et al., 1991, p. 16).

PROBLEMS OF NONCOMPLIANCE

As it became clear that the proportion of mailed-back census forms was low, new problems arose. The problem of noncompliance was centered in large urban areas. Local census offices in urban areas found that their enumerators had very heavy workloads; because the enumerators were only temporary employees with relatively low salaries, this also resulted in high levels of employee turnover.

Many of the areas with high rates of noncompliance with the mailed-out census were low-income neighborhoods where the address lists were of poor quality. Enumerators sometimes felt uncomfortable or unsafe in these areas, and in some local offices falsification of data became a problem (Eriksen et al., 1991, Appendix A, pp. 26, 29).

Census enumerators also had to face another problem: Some persons simply had never heard of the census. A Bureau of the Census survey showed that although 98.5% of non-Hispanic Whites had heard of the 1990 census, only 96.4% of Hispanics, 94.1% of non-Hispanic American Indians, and 89% of non-Hispanic Blacks and Asian/Pacific Islanders had heard of it even well after April 1, 1990.

Those who did not send back census forms often had trouble reading the census form. The census form looked difficult to many respondents. Those whose native language was other than English were about twice as likely (22.9%) to fail to mail back the census form as those whose native language was English (11.7%; see Eriksen et al., 1991, p. 66). Although the 1990 census form was available in a Spanish-language version, everyone else had to answer the English-language version.

Race, Hispanic origin, education, birthplace, and income all affected whether a questionnaire was mailed back. "Other races" had the highest rate of failure to mail it back (24.2%), followed by non-Hispanic Blacks (22.9%), Hispanics (13.0%), and non-Hispanic Whites (10.0%). Those with less than a high school education had the highest noncompliance rate (14.3%).

Income was probably the most interesting predictor of mailing back the census because it was somewhat curvilinear. The best mail-back rates were found among those with household incomes between $20,000 and $49,000 (9.8% failed to mail them back); those with higher incomes had slightly higher rates, and those with lower incomes had rates of about 14.5%.

The Post-Enumeration Survey (PES)

Since 1950, the accuracy of each census has been checked by a large-scale independent survey that attempts to gauge the degree of under-, over-, and misenumeration in the original count. These surveys have served a very important function in evaluating censuses because they show that the patterns of under- and misenumeration differ between races, age groups, and sexes (Advisory Committee on Problems of Census Enumeration, 1972, pp. 25-39; U.S. Bureau of the Census, 1988).

The 1990 *Post-Enumeration Survey* (PES) was the largest and most sophisticated ever, covering about 170,000 housing units in 5,290 blocks. Conducted about 6 months after the original enumeration, it had two subsamples drawn from the same blocks. The E-sample was a reinvestigation of housing units listed in the original enumeration. It was designed to find persons missing from the household census questionnaires and to search for erroneous and missing data, including cases where census takers (or respondents) falsified data.

The second and larger sample, the P-sample, involved interviewing *everyone* who lived on these blocks at the time of the PES (Hogan, 1993, p. 1048). These data were then compared with the data for these blocks from the original enumeration. The Bureau of the Census purposely designed a sample that would oversample blocks from areas with high expected rates of underenumeration.

The PES works on the capture-recapture principle: If the results of independent samples of the same population are compared, we can estimate the size of the "real" population, and also estimate the degree of under-, over-, and misenumeration in the original enumeration of the census. Comparing the P-sample to the original enumeration allows us to estimate the degree of undercount of households on sample blocks. The comparison of the E-sample to the original census enumeration allows the estimation of how many individuals within households were missed (or overcounted), and the estimation of error rates on responses to census questions.

The ability of the PES to measure error rates on different questions is of great benefit to researchers. Though the question of "the under-count" has dominated the coverage of the census in the popular press, the accuracy of responses to census questions is of major interest to researchers.

There were a variety of ways in which persons could be *erroneously enumerated*. They could be double-counted on the same or a nearby block. This could occur in many ways, including one household submitting more than one questionnaire, different family members submitting more than one questionnaire, and so on. This accounted for almost 40% of all erroneous enumerations (see Chart 3.2). Ficti-tious enumerations were responsible for about 4% of these erroneous inclusions. In most cases, these occurred when census takers made up persons on census forms.

A slightly larger proportion (4.5%) of all erroneous inclusions were due to erroneous imputations. When the Bureau of the Census was unable to establish the characteristics of certain individuals, a proce-dure called imputation (whereby the characteristics of a nearby per-son were substituted; see below) was used. Research indicates that about 20% of the time this imputation procedure is incorrect, and about half a million persons should be excluded from the U.S. popu-lation. Geocoding errors (households or individuals are assigned to the wrong place) account for another 8.8% of all erroneous inclusions.

The final and largest category of erroneous inclusions (43.6% of the total, or about 4.4 million people) was the "other" category. This included such errors as including persons dying before or born after the census, or those who, according to rules on residence, should have been counted in another place (U.S. General Accounting Office, 1991b; pp. 4-7).

What led to such high rates of erroneous enumerations? Eriksen et al. (1991, Appendix A, p. 553) found that the month in which the census form was returned affected the rate of erroneous enumeration: The January-April, 1990, rate was 2.8%; May, 6.6%; June, 13.8%; July, 18.8%; and August-December, 28.4%. Because these are national fig-

CHART 3.2. Estimates of the Size of the Undercount and Overcount in the 1990 Census

Total Population Count	247.8 million
Persons Erroneously Included	10.2 million (100.0%)
A. Persons double-counted (same or nearby block)	4.0 million (39.2%)
B. Fictitious enumerations (persons made up)	0.4 million (3.8%)
C. Imputed erroneous enumerated persons	0.5 million (4.5%)
D. Geocoding errors	0.9 million (8.8%)
E. Other erroneous enumerations	4.4 million (43.6%)
Undercount Estimates	
A. Demographic analysis estimate (net undercount rate of 1.8%)	4.7 million
B. Post-Enumeration Survey estimates	
1. July, 1991 PES estimate (net undercount rate of 2.1%)	5.3 million
2. September, 1993 PES estimate (net undercount rate of 1.6%)	4.0 million

SOURCES: Data from Hogan (1993, p. 1054); U.S. General Accounting Office (1991b, p. 6).

ures, the rate of erroneous enumeration in some local areas may have been even higher as the pressures to complete the work by late summer mounted.

Another problem of the census is that persons filling out the questionnaire may skip or refuse to answer some questions. Although census takers were supposed to follow up on these problem cases, it was often difficult to track down these missing answers.

This problem becomes particularly salient to the researcher if different groups failed to answer questions at different rates. Chart 3.3 shows estimates of the missing data rates for key questions asked on the short form of the 1980 and 1990 censuses, and for different racial and ethnic groups for the 1990 census.

These data show that rates of noncompliance (either from skipping or simply missing questions) differ by topic, and that the increase in rates of noncompliance between the 1980 and 1990 censuses differ

CHART 3.3. Missing Data Rates for 1980 and 1990 Census Short-Form
Questions, by Race/Hispanic Origin in 1990

	Hispanic Origin	Marital Status	Relation to Person No. 1	Age	Race	Sex
Total Population						
1980	4.2	1.3	2.1	2.9	1.5	0.8
1990	10.6	3.3	3.3	3.1	2.7	1.9
1990 Census Groups						
White, Non-Hisp.	9.7	2.5	2.5	2.6	1.8	1.5
Black, Non-Hisp.	18.5	6.3	5.9	5.6	3.4	3.5
Asian, Non-Hisp.	9.5	3.8	4.5	3.4	2.5	2.3
Other, Non-Hisp.	9.6	4.0	4.3	3.8	3.6	3.1
Hispanic	8.1	6.1	5.9	4.0	9.5	2.6

SOURCE: Data from Eriksen et al. (1991, Appendix A, pp. 645, 646 combined tables).
NOTE: "Relation to Person No. 1" refers to relationship to the person listed first on the census
form (i.e., the person in whose name the residence is rented or owned).

considerably by topic. For example, the missing data rate for the age
question only increased from 2.9% to 3.1% of all short-form answers
between 1980 and 1990, but the missing responses for the sex question
more than doubled, from 0.8% to 1.9%. The missing data rates also
more than doubled between 1980 and 1990 for the questions on
Hispanic origin and marital status.

Chart 3.3 also shows that race and Hispanic status of persons is also
related to missing data rates. Even though allocation of answers from
other respondents is used to replace such missing answers (see U.S.
Bureau of the Census, 1992e, p. 108), *rates* of allocation can not only
differ by area (see Table 83 of each state's *General Population Characteristics* [U.S. Bureau of the Census, 1992a]) or by question, but also
by characteristics of the respondent. If, for example, 6.3% of all
non-Hispanic Blacks and 6.1% of all Hispanics who returned their
short forms left the marital status question blank, a researcher might
want to err on the side of caution in interpreting shifts in proportions
married for these groups between 1980 and 1990.

The Undercount in 1990

As the news media reported on the delays and increased costs in data collection, they also began to focus on the initial reports on the size of the undercount in 1990 (Choldin, in press). The undercount (i.e., the difference between the number of persons counted in the census and the "true" population size) was thought to have grown between 1980 and 1990. This reversed a 40-year trend toward smaller undercounts in each succeeding census.

In 1990 the undercount initially appeared to be very large for certain areas and groups. This was thought to have the potential for a negative effect on political representation and access to federal dollars apportioned on the basis of population counts (Choldin, in press). Yet later simulation studies showed the undercount would have only a small effect on the redistribution of funds through such "formula programs" (see Murray, 1992; U.S. General Accounting Office, 1991a).

For the researcher, the undercount is troubling because not all of the persons of an area may have been counted. Yet if the undercount was randomly distributed, it would not necessarily bias the results very much. Most researchers are more concerned about whether the undercount is concentrated in certain groups or areas, leading to nonrandom biases in the data and to misinterpretation of results.

When evaluating the data presented below on the undercount, the researcher should not only be comparing them to some absolute standard but also to alternative primary or secondary data collection strategies. Although we know (from the Post-Enumeration Survey) what the 1990 census undercount was, what is the undercount in a telephone survey? Obviously the homeless and precariously housed are missed in telephone surveys; does this limit their effectiveness in the measurement of certain variables or social processes? In other words, researchers should consider the alternatives when weighing the use of census data. Its quality or usefulness can vary considerably according to the specific question asked, social group covered, or location under analysis, but the available data from other sources may sometimes be even worse.

MEASURING THE UNDERCOUNT
IN 1980 AND 1990

The census undercount has received the most attention because it supposedly increased a great deal from 1980 to 1990. The undercount is measured in two ways: through the use of the Post-Enumeration Survey and through *demographic analysis*. In the latter method a variety of demographic techniques are applied to data from prior censuses and measures of births, deaths, and migration from 1980 to 1990 to develop an estimate of the size of the U.S. population at the time of the census count. Any divergence in the size of the population as measured by the actual census count from this simulation model is treated as an overcount or an undercount.

The latest revision of the 1980 census undercount estimated through demographic analysis was 2.8 million out of a total population of 226.5 million. This is an undercount of 1.2% (i.e., demographic analysis projected a population 2.8 million more than the 226.5 million people actually found in 1980; see U.S. General Accounting Office, 1991b, p. 7).

Demographic analysis of the 1990 census indicates that the net undercount was 4.7 million, or 1.8% of the enumerated population of 248.7 million (see Chart 3.2; see also Robinson, Ahmed, Gupta, & Woodrow, 1993, p. 1063). Thus, although the population increased about 9.8% between 1980 and 1990, demographic analysis estimated that the net undercount rose more than 50% (from 1.2% to 1.8%).

COMPARING THE PES AND DEMOGRAPHIC
ANALYSIS ESTIMATES OF THE UNDERCOUNT

The PES can be used to estimate the proportion of undercounted or erroneously enumerated persons in different kinds of areas. Demographic analysis can usually only be used to estimate population undercounts for the entire United States. The PES can also simultaneously estimate the undercount, the erroneously enumerated population, and the proportion of questions answered incorrectly. Demographic analysis can only be used to estimate the *net* undercount (i.e., the difference between the estimated population and the enumerated population, with no estimate of the erroneously enumerated population).

The Bureau of the Census combines data from the Post-Enumeration Survey with the original census data to produce its *dual system estimate* of the size of the U.S. population (Schenker, 1993, p. 1044). This dual system estimate is, like demographic analysis, also an estimate of the degree of undercount in the original census, but the methodology is entirely different.

In July 1991 the official estimate of the undercount based on the PES was 5.3 million people (compared to a demographic analysis estimate of 4.7 million people), or about 2.1% of the population (see Chart 3.2). After further analysis of the data and methods used in the dual system estimate (including discovery of errors in the July 1991 estimates), the current Bureau of the Census 1990 dual system estimate of the undercount is about 1.6%, not 2.1% (an undercount of about 4 million people or about 1.3 million fewer than before; see Hogan, 1993, p. 1054).

These recent data suggest that the 1990 census was considerably more accurate than its critics (and the initial Bureau of the Census estimates) maintained. Although many have suggested that the 1990 undercount was higher than in 1980, the method used to estimate the 1980 undercount (the Post-Enumeration Program, or PEP) differed in many ways from the 1990 PES, so that their estimates of net undercount or erroneous inclusions are not comparable (U.S. General Accounting Office, 1991b, p. 4) and are not presented here.

The undercount in 1990, in terms of absolute numbers and in terms of proportion of the overall population, was *lower* than for any census from 1940 to 1970 (the only censuses for which any realistic estimate of the undercount can be made). Although the undercount grew from 1980 to 1990, the overall 1990 undercount was still probably the second best in history. In addition, the close match in the estimation of the undercount (1.8% by demographic analysis, 1.6% by the dual system estimate) from two unrelated methods suggests that these estimates are close to the truth.

The undercount becomes a major problem for researchers who want to examine census data for certain specific groups. For example, among non-Black Hispanics who lived in large urbanized areas in the Northeast section of the United States, the undercount rate was 0.67% for those who owned their homes, but 6.72% for those who did not (Hogan, 1993, p. 1054). A researcher planning to use census data for an investigation among Hispanic homeowners can probably be far more confident in using unadjusted census data than one using census data on Hispanic renters. In general, the highest rates of undercount are found among men, young adults, minorities, and nonhomeowners.

RESULTS OF THE
UNDERCOUNT CONTROVERSY

Bureau of the Census personnel and outside scholars devoted a large amount of effort to developing and evaluating methodologies for adjusting the 1990 census totals using the PES undercount estimates. As one of her last official acts in December 1992, Director of the Bureau of the Census Barbara Bryant announced that there would be no adjustment of the original 1990 census figures ("Director Announces," 1993, p. 1). This decision ran counter to the opinion of many statisticians and demographers within the Bureau (and also to the view of many on the Committee on the Adjustment of Post-Censal Estimates), who felt that adjusted estimates would improve accuracy at the state and national level (Fay & Thompson, 1993).

As of 1993 all official 1990 census data released by the Bureau of the Census are the original counts. Adjusted counts were prepared for different geographical areas in anticipation of the July 1991 decision by Secretary of Commerce Robert Mossbacher on whether to adjust the 1990 census results. This "unofficial" set of adjusted counts for voting districts (P.L. 94-171 data) supplied to the U.S. House of Representatives by the Bureau of the Census can be obtained from the Inter-University Consortium for Political and Social Research.

Whether Director Bryant's December 1992 memorandum also prevents the use of adjusted figures in the Bureau of the Census's computation of population projections, estimation of measurement error, and other demographic techniques is not clear (this is based on personal communications with a number of Bureau of the Census researchers). In the future some researchers may begin to use the adjusted rather than the "official" census counts in their investigations.

Several major government surveys conducted with Bureau of the Census participation (such as the National Health Interview Survey or the Current Population Survey) may give users the option of using an adjusted or nonadjusted 1990 sampling frame ("Director Announces," 1993, p. 1). Researchers may then have to decide which count is most appropriate for their purposes.

Coding, Cleaning, and Interpretation of Census Data

Since 1960 the Bureau of the Census has used FOSDIC (Film Optical Scanning Device for Input to Computers) to record data from census forms on microfilm and to build electronic files from these data. This involves using data from the original darkened circles on the census form as well as building software routines to input and edit written responses (such as job descriptions). These data are built into geographically based *basic record tapes* (BRTs), which become the sources for all of the census data products provided to the public and for other tabulations used only by Bureau of the Census personnel.

ALLOCATION AND SUBSTITUTION OF MISSING DATA

If there is an obviously bad or missing datum on a question for an individual or household, the Bureau of the Census's computer programs automatically *allocate* an answer that is similar to others in the household or to a unit or person nearby. For example, if the "race" question was not recorded for one person in a household, then that person would be assigned the race of the rest of the household members. Using the so-called hot deck technique, a 30-year-old man with a missing marital status would be assigned the marital status of a randomly chosen 30-year-old man from a nearby household.

If a census form was destroyed, or, as in the case of last resort, closeout, and non–data-defined household units, the information was scarce (or often in error) then the allocation strategy would not produce good results. In this case, *substitution* was used: There was a wholesale assignment of *all* data on a person or household unit from another person or household unit in the same local area.

How frequently did the Bureau of the Census have to use allocation and substitution? In the *General Population Characteristics* volume (see U.S. Bureau of the Census, 1992a) for each state for 1990, Table 83 gives the percentage of all responses with allocation and substitution. For example, in Illinois in 1990, 0.9% of the state's population of 11.4 million (or more than 100,000 people) were "persons substituted for non-interview." Another 17.7% of the population (or more than 2 million people) had one or more of their population items allocated.

Among the most commonly allocated items in Illinois for allocation were race (2.1%), origin (of any race, 11.2%), sex (1.3%), age (2.6%), relationship to householder (2.7%), and marital status (2.1%).

What did the population look like before and after allocation and substitution? Table 82 of the *General Population Characteristics* volume shows the population totals before and after allocation as well as after allocation and substitution. Before allocation and substitution the Bureau of the Census counted about 11,088,000 persons in Illinois. Allocation added 244,000 more (to a total of 11,332,000, or an increase of 2.2%), and allocation and substitution jointly added 343,000 (to 11,431,000 persons), or 3.09% more than the original enumerated population.

How much did allocation and substitution change the characteristics of the population? Before allocation and substitution, 78.9% of the population of Illinois was White and 14.5% was Black. After allocation and substitution, the White proportion dropped slightly (to 78.3%) and the Black proportion rose to 14.8%.

Although allocation and substitution had little effect on the overall proportions of the racial groups in Illinois's total population, they did have a differential effect on the growth of these groups. After allocation and substitution the population of Whites in Illinois grew by 2.3%; Blacks by 5.2%; American Indians, Eskimos, and Aleuts by 4.8%; Asian and Pacific Islanders by 2.9%; and other races (who were heavily Hispanic) by 10.4%.

The patterns of missed housing units and responses varied by race. Yet Table 82 also shows that including allocated and substituted responses has little effect on the population's proportional distribution by sex, age, or marital status.

The Bureau of the Census also reports the proportion of all allocated and substituted responses for each state by total state, level of urbanization, and inside or outside the metropolitan area, county, place, and county subdivision (of 1,000 people or more; see *General Population Characteristics*, Table 83). Thus researchers can tell if there were problems of enumeration in some local areas.

For example, throughout Illinois the proportion of persons substituted for noninterview (i.e., never enumerated) was 0.9%. In most places and county subdivisions this proportion was well under 0.5%. In a few cases it was well over 2%, but the reasons for this are not always clear.

In the village of Forest Park near west suburban Chicago (a lower middle-class suburb once described uncharitably by a local reporter as "Archie Bunker's neighbors"), the proportion of persons substituted for noninterview was 3.3%. In surrounding communities this proportion of nonenumerated persons was far lower: Oak Park was 1.5%, North Riverside was 0.3%, Riverside was 0.1%, and Lyons was 0.2%. There may have been highly localized breakdowns in the census system that resulting in patterns of underenumeration unrelated to the usual effects of urbanization, race, proportion of apartment dwellings versus houses, and other factors influencing underenumeration.

Researchers conducting projects that seek to demonstrate that local areas differ a great deal on certain census characteristics should inspect the proportion of allocated and substituted responses closely. Table 83 of the *General Population Characteristics* shows, for example, that in almost every place in Illinois the most frequently allocated response was "Origin (of any race)" (i.e., the long-form question on ancestry or ethnic origin). Statewide, 11.2% of all answers were allocated, and in many places more than 15% of all answers were allocated. This high level of allocation on this question suggests that this variable may be a less than ideal one for detailed local area comparisons because so many failed to answer it, and because the patterns of nonresponse were not consistent across the state.

SUPPRESSION, CONFIDENTIALITY, AND DATA THRESHOLDS

Since the mid-19th century, the Bureau of the Census has been required by law to keep census records confidential (Halacy, 1980, pp. 138-144). There are several possible ways confidentiality could be violated, and the Bureau of the Census has different strategies to deal with them.

One obvious way in which confidentiality could be violated is disclosure of data from census forms by enumerators or in the process of coding or compilation of data. Since 1910 there have been laws against disclosure of information on individuals, households, and, for business censuses, on business establishments (Kaplan et al., 1980, pp. 68-71).

In recent years local governments have challenged the accuracy of census counts in their areas. In 1980, for example, New York City and state officials attempted to force the Bureau of the Census to supply them with names and addresses of enumerated persons. They could then challenge its enumeration counts by showing that large numbers of persons were missed, and that the city and state were unfairly deprived of their shares of federal resources and legislative seats during the reapportionment process. Using a defense based on Federal statutes, Bureau of the Census procedures, and the Privacy Act of 1974, Bureau of the Census lawyers were able to argue successfully before the Supreme Court that such disclosure could not be permitted (Mitroff, Mason, & Barabba, 1983, pp. 15-16, 93-96).

Once data have been compiled, however, it may also be possible to identify individuals, households, or families through the cross-tabulation of census results. Since 1930 it has also been illegal for the Bureau of the Census to publish tabulations of data in which individuals, households, or business establishments can be identified (Kaplan et al., 1980, p. 69).

The Bureau of the Census has taken several steps to prevent the identification of individuals or households from statistical tables created for the 1990 census. Because they differ slightly from procedures used in earlier censuses, they deserve some attention.

Suppression. When a group analyzed in a table includes only a small number of persons, the Bureau of the Census may suppress the data through the use of a *threshold*. Where race is cross-classified with other variables the Bureau of the Census uses table thresholds that specify that a certain number of members of a racial group must be in the geographic area before data will be reported for that racial group. Although the 1980 threshold level was generally 400 persons of the specific group, the 1990 thresholds are more variable (cf. Myers, 1992, p. 72).

For example, in Table 66 of *General Population Characteristics: Illinois,* "Household and Family Characteristics for Selected Racial Groups: 1990" (see U.S. Bureau of the Census, 1992a), the number of Asian and Pacific Islanders are reported for different places in the state. The threshold level for this table is 400, so only racial groups with at least this number of persons in the area will be included.

In the city of Chicago all of the major Asian groups (All Asian, Chinese, Filipino, Japanese, Asian Indian, Korean, and Vietnamese) are cross-classified by age, sex, and so on. Guamanians (713 of whom live in Chicago) get a separate listing, but because there were fewer than 400 Samoans or Hawaiians, their totals are included in the broader All Pacific Islander category, which is cross-classified with the descriptive variables. In Table 66, several smaller Asian groups

(Cambodian, Laotian, and Thai) that were "write-in" answers to the general Asian/Pacific Islander race question response are also cross-classified by other variables because each group had more than 400 inhabitants in Chicago.

In smaller places the selected racial group might only be All Asian (if there were at least 400 total Asians), or All Asian and one or more constituent Asian groups. For example, for North Chicago (a separate city), Table 66 of the *General Population Characteristics* lists the All Asian total as 1,195 and the Filipino population as 912. Thus there were a total of 283 non-Filipino Asians in North Chicago city, but the table does not allow us to tell to what Asian groups they belong.

The Bureau of the Census also uses a *complementary threshold* "to limit the presentation of characteristics for the White population when the population of races other than White is small and for the White, not of Hispanic origin population when the Hispanic origin population is small" (U.S. Bureau of the Census, 1992a, p. III-1). Hence some data on the White population or the White, non-Hispanic population are suppressed if the non-White or Hispanic White groups are so small that the total population figures are close to the totals for Whites or non-Hispanic Whites.

Thresholds and complementary thresholds vary from 250 to 1,000 persons, depending on the table. For researchers planning on using printed census volumes to look at characteristics of racial groups who are only a small minority of the inhabitants of any area, these levels may be important barriers to research.

For example, 231,768 Asians or Pacific Islanders in Illinois live in places where they comprise at least 400 or more persons; this is only 81.2% of all of the population of this racial group (which totals 285,311 persons) for the entire state. The 19% of Asians and Pacific Islanders who live in places where they constitute only a small racial minority may well have different social or economic characteristics than those who live in more concentrated groups; however, their local area characteristics cannot be ascertained from Bureau of the Census publications.

NEW CONFIDENTIALITY EDITS FOR 1990

As noted above, the Bureau of the Census has a legal responsibility to prevent the disclosure of data on individuals and households in its tabulations. In the 1990 census a new procedure was developed whereby certain variables on similar households in different parts of a state were swapped. "The result is that a small amount of uncertainty is introduced into some of the census characteristics to prevent identification of specific individuals, households or housing units" (U.S. Bureau of the Census, 1992a, p. C-1).

This interchanging of variables is done between a sample of households and individuals within a state. It does not affect the total counts for all persons, Hispanic origin, American Indian tribe, race, and total of all persons 18 years and over. To protect the confidentiality of those in small areas, their confidentiality edit sample is proportionately larger.

The Bureau of the Census developed this procedure to meet two competing demands: the statutory requirement for protection of the privacy of individuals in the publication of data, and the need to produce more specific data for small areas. What does it mean for the researcher? There is a very small degree of nonsampling error introduced into 100% count census data. As a result, census data and analyses of census data are very slightly less accurate than they might be.

The obvious trade-off here is that because the Bureau of the Census provides data at much lower levels of aggregation, analyses of census data can be more accurate because they can be conducted at lower levels. Finally, as this and the next chapter demonstrate, there are so many other sources of nonsampling error that the added error due to confidentiality edits is of little consequence.

CONFIDENTIALITY IN THE PUMS

The Public Use Microdata Samples (PUMS), the 5% and 1% samples of complete household- and individual-level data from the long form of the census, could possibly be used to identify specific households and individuals in local communities. Therefore the Bureau of the Census only locates households in these samples within relatively broad geographic areas.

The 5% sample of households only categorizes households by geographic units of at least 100,000 persons. Because many counties have populations of less than 100,000 the geographic unit used to identify these PUMS households is the *county group*, a group of adjacent counties with an aggregate population of at least 100,000 persons. In cases where the county population is at least 100,000, the PUMS household is assigned directly to that county.

The other PUMS file, the 1% of households in *Metropolitan Statistical Areas* (MSAs), will also only permit the identification of households at the MSA level. Because the minimum population of MSAs is 100,000 (75,000 in New England), levels of confidentiality in the 1% PUMS are similar to the 5% PUMS.

Many researchers now want to use PUMS data to link areal and individual- (or household-) level data in a contextual analysis format (see Iverson, 1991). The PUMS confidentiality rules mean, however, that individuals or households *cannot* be linked with small geographic areas, only with large counties, county groups, or MSAs.

Hence it is important to consider whether independent areal or contextual variables that could be used (the crime rate, poverty rate, index of racial segregation, economic growth rate, etc.) are applicable to households or individuals who could live *anywhere* in the area. Researchers should be wary of using contextual variables that might have a very uneven distribution across a county group or an MSA to explain individual- or household-level phenomena.

INTERPRETATION AND SCALING OF CENSUS DATA

The Bureau of the Census must make complex decisions on the appropriate indices or categories to apply to data from areas, households, families, and individuals. This problem is particularly acute in the presentation of data on income. Ideally it would be very useful to be able to use the same income categories in 1990 as were used in 1980 or 1970. Because of inflation, however, a $30,000 annual income does not mean the same thing in terms of purchasing power in 1990, 1980, and 1970 (see Levy, 1987).

A similar problem exists for the compilation of data on the distribution of poverty. The "poverty line" or "poverty rate" has, since its inception in 1964, been meant to be an *absolute* measure of poverty: It refers to a family or individual income level where one third or more of all income must be spent for a subsistence level of food (see *Summary Social, Economic and Housing Characteristics* [U.S. Bureau of the Census, 1992i], Appendix, pp. B-27-8, 43; see also Jencks, 1991, pp. 32-36). It must, however, be computed for each family (or individual living apart from other family members), and several other factors (presence of children, age, and size of family) must also be factored in before it can be determined whether or not a family or nonfamily individual is above or below the poverty line.

Once the number of *families* with incomes below the poverty line is computed, it is then possible to see how many constituent members of these families (such as children) fall below the poverty line. Because the Bureau of the Census treats income as a *shared* characteristic in the computation of the poverty line, it is necessary to compute it first at the group (i.e., family) level, then redistribute it among individuals.

For example, census data for Illinois show that 264,413 families had 1989 incomes that fell below the poverty line (U.S. Bureau of the Census, 1992i, p. 279). Thus 9.0% of all families in Illinois fell below the poverty line. For all *individuals* in Illinois for whom poverty status could be determined (i.e., excluding those in prisons, long-term hospitals, etc.), 11.9% were in poverty. These figures would seem to indicate that family membership leads to a lower risk of poverty.

Yet when the number of "related children" (i.e., children in families) who were members of families below the poverty line is summed, a different picture emerges. For related children under 18 years, 485,706 (or 16.8% of all related children under 18) were in poverty. Thus the poverty rate for related children under age 18 is 7.8% higher than the poverty rate for families as a whole, and 4.9% higher than the rate of poverty for all individuals in the state. Children in families (and this excludes foster children, not a notably high-income group) appear to be receiving no particular protection from poverty from their family membership. This kind of useful information can only emerge if group characteristics (in this case, the poverty rates for families) are computed and attached to individuals (here, related children under age 18).

Many of these derived measures are also attached to areas. For example, the Bureau of the Census computes a "median selected monthly owner costs as a percentage of household income in 1989" for both mortgaged and nonmortgaged housing units (see U.S. Bureau of the Census, 1992i, Table 15). For each owner household, data on monthly owner costs (the sum of costs, including mortgages, real estate taxes, utilities, insurance, etc.) is divided by household income.

The *median percentage* of this household indicator is then computed for the geographic area in question. For the state of Illinois as a whole, owner costs for housing units with mortgages are 20.2% of household income, while owner costs for that fortunate minority without mortgages (about 28% of all owner-occupied units statewide) had a median value of 12.7% of household income (U.S. Bureau of the Census, 1992i, p. 451).

The median monthly owner costs of mortgaged housing units were $1,067 (or 22.4% of median household income in 1989) in Dupage County, an affluent suburb of Chicago. By comparison, median monthly owner costs were $840 in Cook County (which includes the city of Chicago and the more urbanized suburbs), or 20.9% of 1989 median household income. DuPage County property owners paid almost $200 a month more for housing, yet in relation to their income these costs were only 1.5% more than those of Cook County owners. These data suggest that a researcher looking at the origins of the suburban property tax revolt might study the literature on relative as opposed to actual deprivation.

USE OF CONFIDENCE INTERVALS WITH SAMPLE CENSUS DATA

Many of the more interesting questions in the 1990 census were obtained on a sample basis on the long form. Compared to most sample surveys, the census sample proportion was very large (often as many as one out of every two households), but these questions are still subject to *sampling error.*

For census data, determining the amount of sampling error is a complex topic, because the census varies the proportional size of the sample by kind of place (rural areas are sampled more heavily) and because a variety of weighting techniques are used as well. Fortunately for the user, directions on how to compute standard errors for sample census data expressed as totals, percentages, sums, differences, ratios, and medians are given in Appendix C of each state's *Summary Social, Economic and Housing Characteristics* (1990 CPH-5) volume (U.S. Bureau of the Census, 1992i).

Summary Social, Economic and Housing Characteristics also gives some useful examples of previously computed standard errors that may place this problem in a more comprehensible context. Table 19 (Percent in Sample, Standard Error, and Confidence Bounds for Population Characteristics), for example, shows that among the 11.4 million persons in Illinois, 15.3% received the sample (long) form of the census (*Summary Social, Economic and Housing Characteristics* [U.S. Bureau of the Census, 1992i], p. 514).

Table 19 also shows that the standard error of per capita income in 1989 was 15 dollars (see column 3). From Table 9 in the same volume, we know that the per capita income in 1989 was $15,201 (see column

1, *Summary Social, Economic and Housing Characteristics* [U.S. Bureau of the Census, 1992i], p. 279). By multiplying the standard error (here, $15) by 1.96 (see the z-score table in any introductory statistics textbook), the 95% confidence interval limits can be obtained. Thus the 95% confidence interval for per capita income per person in Illinois is $15,172 to $15,230.

When an area's total population or sampling proportion is small, the standard error of estimate increases dramatically. With very small areal units and small sampling proportions it can increase so much (and the confidence intervals become so wide) that the null hypothesis that there is no difference between places for a particular variable cannot be rejected (due to overlapping confidence intervals).

For example, in Adams County, Illinois, there are two adjacent townships, Beverly (population 363 in 1990) and McKee (population 205). Beverly's per capita income was $12,942 in 1989 and McKee's was $10,563. Beverly Township's sampling fraction for the long form of the census was 8.8%, and McKee Township's was 12.2%.

The combination of a small population and a very low sampling fraction gave Beverly Township a wide per capita income standard error of $2,311, or a 95% confidence interval of $10,631 to $15,252. McKee Township had a standard error of $2,048, and a confidence interval of $8,515 to $12,611. The overlaps in their confidence intervals made it impossible (at the 95% level) to reject the null hypothesis of *no difference* in their per capita income levels, even though initially Beverly's Township's appeared to be more than $2,300 higher.

Many researchers tend to disregard the problem of confidence intervals in sample census data and treat them as if they are the same as population data. They are not, and when the size of the sampled population gets below about 600 to 800 persons (see diagram in Myers, 1992, p. 85) the confidence interval can widen rapidly. In addition, some sample population characteristics have wider or narrower confidence intervals due to the sample's *design factors* (see *Summary Social, Economic, and Housing Characteristics* [U.S. Bureau of the Census, 1992i], pp. C-2, C-11).

Finally, as the Bureau of the Census warns, computing the confidence intervals only covers the problem of sampling errors; it does not take account of a variety of nonsampling errors. Obviously, many researchers would prefer to ignore such problems as undercoverage or respondent or enumerator error. Yet researchers should be aware of the limits and problems in the use of census data as they prepare research designs, choose statistical methods, and evaluate the results and significance of their studies.

4. Preparing Data for Analysis

How can 1990 census data be used in specific research projects? This chapter endeavors to answer this very broad question by giving two examples of social science research that used census data. Because the kinds of available data and computer hardware and software have changed since these research projects were completed (both used 1980 census data), the focus here is on how these projects could be undertaken using current census data and computer technology.

Two kinds of census data have been used in examples of census research given here: those using geographic data and those using the Public Use Microdata Samples (PUMS). Geographically based census data can yield a great deal of specific information about areas, but census confidentiality rules prohibit the identification of individuals or households within those areas.

PUMS data provide highly specific data on households, families, and individuals but are restricted geographically. These households can only be located in an area containing at least 100,000 persons, not in neighborhoods or smaller areas. As a result, it is often difficult to link community- or ecologically based variables to the data from these persons. These restrictions make it important for researchers using census data to formulate their hypotheses with special attention as to whether they are specifying ecological or individual relationships.

An Areal Example:
Neighborhood Racial Succession, 1970-1980

Barrett A. Lee and Peter B. Wood (1991) examined a key problem in the ecology of modern American cities: Does the succession model work? This model of urban change, used by many urban analysts, has attempted to explain residential "tipping"; the idea that once a significant number of Blacks move into a neighborhood various institutional factors and decisions by homeowners result in the rapid exit of Whites and a transition to a resegregated neighborhood, albeit of a different race.

Lee and Wood were examining a theory that was more concerned with what would happen to *neighborhoods* once they reached a certain proportion Black than with *individual-level* behavior. The only way to test the theory was with areal data; individual and household census data would not shed much light on the process of neighborhood succession because PUMS data only allow the location of each household in a "neighborhood" of at least 100,000 persons.

Once they had decided on this approach, Lee and Wood next had to define what they meant by *neighborhood* and especially by *mixed neighborhood*. They also had to decide whether they were going to use data from just one city, one region, or the entire United States in order to test their theory. Their operationalization of succession theory was the degree to which neighborhoods' racial composition at one point in time (i.e., in 1970) was related to racial composition a decade later.

Because the succession model was developed for urban areas, Lee and Wood picked neighborhoods from 58 of the 60 central cities across the United States with populations of 250,000 or more in 1970 or 1980. The census tract was used as their measure of a neighborhood, and they defined a "mixed neighborhood" as one with a 1970 population between 10% and 89% Black. Due to the high level of residential segregation in the United States, only slightly more than 20% of all central city census tracts (2,259 in all) qualified as mixed tracts (Lee & Wood, 1991, p. 24).

To test the theory, it was necessary to find data on the percentage Black in the census tract in 1970 and 1980. This meant that they had to use the Summary Tape Files (STF) for both of these census years, obtain the relevant census tract variables (i.e., the total populations by race), then match the tract data for 1970 and 1980. In order to clarify the neighborhood comparison they also excluded census tracts with fewer than 500 residents in either census year (tracts usually have about 4,000 inhabitants), tracts with a majority of their population in group quarters, and tracts that had major boundary changes between 1970 and 1980 (Lee & Wood, 1991).

Lee and Wood show that succession (where tracts turn from White to Black) is not the overwhelming pattern in 1980 for all mixed census tracts in 1970. In fact, in cities in the western United States, only about a third of mixed tracts underwent succession by 1980; one third experienced stability (the proportions of Whites and Blacks stayed roughly the same), and one third experienced displacement (where the proportion of Blacks in the mixed census tract declined). The authors proceed to analyze the phenomenon at the level of individual cities, then look at some of the independent variables that seem to be important predictors of whether or not a census tract stays integrated, becomes all Black, or turns largely White again.

This article is easily understandable to anyone with even an elementary grasp of multivariate statistics. It is elegant because it uses a relatively simple measure (the change in percentage of Black residents in mixed-race census tracts between 1970 and 1980) to suggest that the scholarly literature on succession has perhaps mistakenly assumed that the phenomenon will happen everywhere in much the same way.

Their findings demonstrate that there are important regional differentials in the process. In the spirit of the original Chicago School literature on succession, Lee and Wood suggest that we should spend more time looking at why succession occurs in some places (and not in others) rather than assuming that neighborhoods will inexorably become heavily minority once even a small proportion of Blacks move in.

The 1990 census data will provide a similar data set (census tract data with variables largely similar to the 1980 ones) for the extension of this line of research. As Dowell Myers (1992) has shown, relatively simple comparisons of local census tract data can often show some very interesting trends in population and housing characteristics that do not become apparent until the data from earlier and later censuses are compared. The Lee and Wood article is also satisfying because they study a time-dependent ecological process—succession—and measure it with units that remain basically the same over time.

A researcher interested in replicating Lee and Wood's research using 1990 census data would probably want to do so using data from either CD-ROM or from magnetic tape. Uploading the data necessary (i.e., data on all census tracts) for determining the number of mixed (or integrated) census tracts in 60 major American cities from CD-ROM would not be a trivial task. Determining the number of all mixed tracts is not a complex process (in fact, it could even be done on a spreadsheet rather than a statistical analysis program), but on a personal computer it would also take some time. The regression equation performed across the mixed tracts (with about 2,300 units) could be performed rapidly with a statistical analysis package on a 386- or higher level personal computer.

The data necessary for this analysis could also be obtained from a magnetic tape (or tape cartridge) of STF-1A, the tape that gives totals by race at the census tract level. A program to extract the data from the STF-1A must be written (see, e.g., Myers, 1992, pp. 343-345) and must specify what level of geography (in this case, census tracts) and what variables are needed. Variables on STF-1A are arranged by numbered fields or table (matrix) numbers (see U.S. Bureau of the Census, 1991, pp. 13-22); total number of persons is in Table P1 at positions 301-309, persons by race (broad racial categories) is in Table P7 at positions 382-426, and so on.

Again, mounting all of the magnetic tapes necessary to strip off the data needed for census tracts for 60 cities (these tapes are available by state) is not a trivial project, even at a large computer center. Much of the rest of the project (the computation of the variables, running the descriptive statistics and the regression equations, and so on) will be very similar whether it is run from CD-ROM to a personal computer or from magnetic tape to a mainframe computer account.

At present there is no clear answer as to whether it is quicker and easier to run a project of this kind from a mainframe or a personal computer or to download the data from CD-ROMs or from magnetic tapes or cartridges. If you are at an institution with a large mainframe computer, lots of programming help, and easy access to the ICPSR versions of the STF or PUMS tapes (which are already set up as SAS or SPSS variables), then it probably makes sense to use tapes and a mainframe computer. If you are working for a community organization with only a personal computer and access to a library with census CD-ROMs that can be downloaded to floppy disks, then the other route looks more practical.

An Individual-Level Analysis Example

Why is the rate of unemployment so high among Black urban youth? Several kinds of explanations have been offered, but they generally propose that (a) among these youth, there exists a weak orientation toward and attachment with the world of work; (b) there is discrimination against young Black workers by employers; or (c) job opportunities have moved to the suburbs, making it difficult for inner-city minority youth to find them or to commute there (Ihlanfeldt & Sjoquist, 1990, p. 274). Hypotheses (b) and (c) are sometimes contrasted as the "race" and "space" explanations and have been identified with the work of David Ellwood and John Kain (and more recently John Kasarda), respectively.

Ihlanfeldt and Sjoquist (1990) decided to test the extent to which the race or space hypotheses explained the rates of labor force participation in the Philadelphia metropolitan area. They wanted to test if the time it took to commute to work (a variable available from the census) affected the probability of labor force participation and whether the effect was different for Black and White youth. They were interested in how much of the difference in labor force participation rates between 16- to 19- and 20- to 24-year-old Blacks and Whites was due to poor location (i.e., Blacks tended to be located in areas far from many jobs) and how much was due to what might be called true racial factors (employer discrimination, etc.).

The authors used the 1980 Public Use Sample (PUS, equivalent of the 1990 PUMS) to test their hypothesis. For planning purposes, the 1980 PUS data from Philadelphia was divided into 26 districts, so it was possible to obtain a 6% (i.e., the A and B) sample for each of these districts.

One innovative aspect of Ihlanfeldt and Sjoquist's work was how they computed their key independent variable, the job location indicator. They used the mean time it took employed young people in each of these 26 districts to get to work as the indicator of the degree of difficulty in commuting to a job (they computed this mean commuting time separately for Black and White youth in each district).

In estimating a partial derivative model to explain the probability of having a job among the Black and White Philadelphia youth in the PUS, they assigned this mean commuting time for the district to each young person in the district. Their results showed that it did matter whether someone lived in a district with good or bad job access. In Philadelphia, they claim, "from 33 to 54 percent of the gap [in youth employment rates between races] can be attributed to space, depending on the group considered" (Ihlanfeldt & Sjoquist, 1990, p. 268).

Ihlanfeldt and Sjoquist put heavy emphasis on individual analysis. They suggest that one reason why their findings differ from the earlier work of David Ellwood is that they have better individual-level measurement of these variables, whereas Ellwood often used census tract-level analysis (Ihlanfeldt & Sjoquist, 1990, p. 274). Clearly, some mixture of areal and individual data is needed to measure job access (partly because the unemployed do not have any commuting time to report), but the authors make a fairly convincing case that here it makes more sense to use individual-level PUS data rather than performing an analysis of differences between areal units.

At the end of their article (p. 275) Ihlanfeldt and Sjoquist give a list of the variables that they used from the 1980 PUS. In many ways the logic of using the PUS or the 1990 PUMS is not much different from the logic of social survey inquiry taught in many graduate-level statistics and research methods courses. What gives the Ihlanfeldt and Sjoquist article a clever twist is their assignment of these Philadelphia young people to good or bad "job access districts," the inclusion of this factor as an explanatory variable, the transracial statistical comparisons, and a clear statement of the theoretical implications of their work.

In this research project the authors first had to select individuals who fit their criteria (by place of residence, age, and race). They thus greatly decreased the size of the sample from 6% (they added the PUS A and B samples together) of all Philadelphia residents to a sample perhaps only one fifth to one tenth this size (i.e., a sample of about 50,000 young people).

A sample of this size is still probably best analyzed on a mainframe computer. Personal computers can now handle large case bases quite rapidly, but many PUMS files will simply be too large for them to handle efficiently. Of course, if a smaller PUMS sampling fraction is used or if the PUMS is taken from a small area (such as from one county or county group of 100,000 persons) then it may be practical to use a personal computer for analysis. For most PUMS users, however, a mainframe computer (or perhaps a workstation) will suit their needs better, especially in the earlier stages of the analysis, when large databases are often reduced to the smaller groups of interest.

Should Ecological or Individual-Level Comparisons Be Made?

Most social scientists (except those trained in the ecological tradition) almost instinctively prefer individual-level comparisons. Most of us have at least heard of the ecological fallacy and the problem of inferring characteristics of individuals from those of areas.

Even so, we do live in a nation where moving even a few miles (or sometimes even a few blocks) can result in huge differences in life chances. If researchers like Kasarda, Massey, or Ihlanfeldt and Sjoquist are right, then distance from needed resources and opportunities or degrees of segregation should be factored into individual-level models, because space or distance may have very important explanatory effects.

In fact, much of the most theoretically interesting work in the sociology of race and stratification uses census data because they are the only source from which microlevel ecological processes *and* individual-level analyses (from PUMS data) can both be derived.

These two examples (and both really deserve to be read in their entirety) show that it is possible to use census data to test important hypotheses in a clear and logical fashion. The expanded range of data products from the 1990 census gives the researcher a number of choices about how to obtain and use the data. If even a cursory investigation of available census data sources and available hardware and software is made, the researcher can frequently save a lot of money and time in the long run.

5. Conclusion

New Data From 1990 and Beyond

The Bureau of the Census will create new data products from the 1990 census that will be released in the future. In addition, technological advances may allow it to release other data sets in new media. For example, none of the pre-1990 publicity releases mentioned that data from the most recent census would be released on magnetic tape cartridges as well as on magnetic tape and CD-ROM.

Researchers can keep up to date with new census data products through two monthly Bureau of the Census periodicals, the *Monthly*

Product Announcement and *Census and You*. New data product information is also found on the Bureau's on-line data system, CENDATA, carried on CompuServe and DIALOG. The most recent edition of the *Census Catalog and Guide* (released each summer) also gives descriptions (including available media and price) of data products.

Some researchers will be interested in developing studies that also use future census data. As the comparison of 1980 and 1990 census topics, questionnaire categories, and geography has shown, these changes can have profound effects on studies of social change.

About the only certain prediction for the year 2000 census is that it will be different from the 1990 one. No one was very satisfied with the results from the last census, and there is a general consensus that new methods and strategies have to be developed to meet the challenge of counting a highly mobile population that, in many instances, has little or no interest in being counted.

Usually, agents of change are on the outside, trying to influence a bureaucracy that is relatively set in its ways. Right now, the picture at the Bureau of the Census is different. Many of the more innovative suggestions are coming from the Bureau's professional staff, and there is great interest in developing enumeration and estimation strategies that will not repeat the mistakes of 1990.

There are currently a large number of "design alternatives" for the year 2000 census (Beresford, 1993). They include giving persons the option to respond by mail or telephone, targeting hard-to-reach populations, putting more stress on the use of preexisting administrative records, and so on.

It appears that the Bureau of the Census is legally obligated (by the Constitution and by the Voting Rights Act) to collect the number of persons by race and Hispanic origin down to the block level. This could, however, be done by a "postcard census" or a similar simple enumeration technique.

Beyond this there is great debate on how accurate and representative data should be collected. Some analysts suggest the greater use of administrative data, whereas others suggest more intensive attempts to find previously underenumerated populations. The more extensive use of statistical estimation procedures and models has also been proposed. Still other researchers say that very large samples (i.e., about the size of the 1990 long form, covering perhaps 15% of the population) on different topics (housing, employment, etc.) could be used to create useful in-depth data that could be applied to local areas.

During the mid-1990s these design alternatives will be tested and evaluated by Bureau of the Census and other government and outside advisory groups. Researchers interested in discovering how the Year 2000 census will be run should read the *Federal Register*, the deliberations of the Advisory Committee of the Year 2000 Task Force, and nongovernmental publications (such as the *APDU Newsletter* or *American Demographics)* that may have articles on this topic.

Where to Learn More
About the 1990 Census

Any researcher with a serious interest in the 1990 census would be well advised to purchase several key documents on the organization and structure of census data. They are (with approximate 1993 prices):

U.S. Bureau of the Census. 1992. *CPH-R-1A. 1990 Census of Population and Housing: Guide. Part A. Text.* ($11.00). This is the best introduction to the technical side of the census: questions asked, census procedures and geography, availability of data products, understanding census categories and statistics, other sources of assistance, and so on. Its companion volume, *Guide. Part B. Glossary* ($5.50), is a worthwhile investment due to its more extensive definitions of Bureau of the Census terminology.

U.S. Bureau of the Census. 1992. *Census Catalog and Guide.* ($22.00). Issued annually since 1985, it covers all Bureau of the Census publications, including descriptions of data products from the censuses of business, government, and agriculture and large-scale surveys (such as the Current Population Survey). It includes information on current availability of data, in what media they are offered (tape, CD-ROM, etc.), and how they can be ordered.

Myers, Dowell. 1992. *Analysis With Local Census Data: Portraits of Change.* ($38.00). A key resource for those interested in population and housing at the local level. It gives very good examples of how to use geographic census micro-data to show these changes.

Finding Prior Research on Census Topics

How does the researcher determine whether a possible research question involving census data can be analyzed at all? More importantly, is this possible research question located within a research tradition that has its own standards of theoretical progress, measurement of concepts, and proof?

The first stage in reading the previous research is to decide what *general area* one's study might fall into—immigration, housing, social stratification, social epidemiology, and so on. Next, it is worthwhile to specify the group or groups to be studied: persons who migrated from Central America in the 1980s, workers in manufacturing industries, currently married women who have graduated from college, and so on.

One of the classic problems facing both the student and the more advanced researcher is that he or she has a rough idea of an interesting research topic but no clear idea of how to check whether or not a question has been analyzed by another researcher.

Research methods textbooks are surprisingly skimpy on the question of how to avoid unknowingly duplicating past research (see, e.g., Frankfort-Nachmias & Nachmias, 1992; Hessler, 1992). Replications of prior studies, especially ones that confirm the original research, are very difficult to publish in the social sciences. It is crucial not to duplicate another's research unwittingly but rather to progress beyond it.

The Russell Sage Foundation has published a series of census monographs on the 1980 census that treat substantive areas of social science or specific groups of interest. These monographs were prepared by experts in each area and are an excellent place to start for anyone who wants to know how data from a variety of census sources can be applied to theoretically significant issues. A list of these monographs is given in Chart 5.1.

These monographs treat their topics from a number of different viewpoints and use a variety of methods and data sources (from inside and outside the census) to make their points (see the reviews of these volumes by Cherlin, 1991a; Choldin & Logan, 1991; C. Goldscheider, 1991; F. K. Goldscheider, 1991). Although the volumes emphasize the statistical description of social trends and more general theoretical lines of argument (rather than hypothesis-testing), they provide ex-

CHART 5.1. The Russell Sage Foundation's Census Monograph Series on the Population of the United States in the 1980s

---

Adams, J. S. (1988). *Housing America in the 1980s.*

Alonso, W., & Starr, P. (Eds.). (1987). *The politics of numbers.*

Barringer, H., Gardner, R. W., & Levin, M. J. (1993). *Asians and Pacific Islanders in the United States.*

Bean, F. D., & Tienda, M. (1988). *The Hispanic population of the United States.*

Bianchi, S. M., & Spain, D. (1986). *American women in transition.*

Farley, R., & Allen, W. R. (1987). *The color line and the quality of life in America.*

Frey, W. H., & Speare, A., Jr. (1988). *Regional and metropolitan growth and decline in the United States.*

Fuguitt, G. V., Brown, D. L., & Beale, C. L. (1987). *Rural and small town America.*

Hernandez, D. J. (1993). *America's children: Resources from family, government and the economy.*

Jasso, G., & Rosenweig, M. R. (1990). *The new chosen people: Immigrants to the United States.*

Levy, F. (1987). *Dollars and dreams: The changing American income distribution.*

Lieberson, S., & Waters, M. C. (1988). *From many strands: Ethnic and racial groups in contemporary America.*

Long, L. (1988). *Migration and residential mobility in the United States.*

Siegel, J. S. (1993). *A generation of change: A profile of America's older population.*

Snipp, C. M. (1989). *American Indians: The first of this land.*

Sweet, J. A., & Bumpass, L. L. (1988). *American families and households.*

White, M. J. (1988). *America's neighborhoods and residential differentiation.*

---

cellent examples of how to condense census data into useful tabular form and how to intersperse textual argument with statistical proof.

The Russell Sage Foundation is also planning a similar series of monographs for the 1990 census under the general editorship of Reynolds Farley. At present it appears that it will be a three- or four-volume effort. Volume 1 will cover social and economic trends in the 1980s, including such topics as changes in household composition, population geography, educational attainment, labor force participation, location of employment, distribution of income, and housing and homelessness. Volume 2 will be on social diversity in the United States and cover changing gender roles, welfare of children and youth, demographics of the older population, racial and ethnic diversity, and the consequences of the new immigration. Volume 3 will be a summary volume for nondemographers that distills the key findings of the studies in Volumes 1 and 2, and Volume 4 will be a companion volume on the population of Puerto Rico.

Completed monographs are to be submitted by the end of 1993, and the first two volumes should be available in early 1995 (Nancy

Cunniff, personal communication, March 30, 1993). As with the 1980 Census Monograph series, these books should be excellent, up-to-date sources of information on these topics.

A one-volume introduction to demographic research using current and historical census data is Donald J. Bogue's *The Population of the United States: Historical Trends and Future Projections* (1985). Bogue's monograph includes many definitions and formulas and may be easier for the nonspecialist to grasp. An updated edition of this work using 1990 census and other demographic data is under preparation by Douglas L. Anderton, Richard E. Barrett, and Donald J. Bogue, and is scheduled for publication in early 1996.

Researchers also have access to two excellent bibliographic sources of reference: *Population Index* and the *Social Science Citation Index*. The *Population Index* (published quarterly) is particularly valuable because it is organized by subject of research (the topical schema is given at the beginning of each issue). Its Geographical Index (at the end of each issue) allows one to cross-reference the topical index by country. Thus one can quickly discover whether there were any studies on population censuses and registers in the United States (16 such studies were covered in the Fall 1992 issue) or internal migration in the United States (five studies were covered in the same issue). Each cited study also includes a short abstract, which is a great aid in attempting to discover whether the book or article is worth reading.

The *Social Science Citation Index* is of use in finding citations by subject or author. It often requires much more time to sift through them, however, and it does not include abstracts. Because it also gives a listing of all of the recent *citations* of an article, it is an excellent way of reconstructing trends in scholarly research.

The best source for articles on a wide variety of census topics is *Demography*. A British journal, *Population Studies*, also publishes articles based on census data or covering methodological problems in census data, as does, more infrequently, the French journal *Population* (these articles are often in English).

The major journals in sociology (*American Sociological Review, American Journal of Sociology, Social Forces*) and in economics (such as the *American Economic Review*) frequently publish substantive articles based on census data, as do journals in urban studies (such as *Urban Affairs Quarterly*). Articles in more specialized journals (such as *Journal of Marriage and the Family, Journal of Family History*, or *International Migration Review*) are sometimes based on PUMS or other census data.

Since the census of 1850 the American Statistical Association has had a profound influence on the ways in which census data are collected and the methods by which errors and bias were detected (Anderson, 1988, pp. 36-37). Articles on the census can be found in the *Journal of the American Statistical Association,* and particularly in its *Proceedings of the Social Statistics Section* (see especially the special census volume of 1991).

If one's research requires highly technical information, the Bureau of the Census's *Annual Research Conference Proceedings* often can provide useful information. These conferences have been held since 1985 and include papers (and discussants' comments) by governmental and nongovernmental specialists on census data. These specialists are often given access to census data that are, for a variety of reasons (most commonly confidentiality rules), not made available to the general public.

A Final Word

Trying to describe the entire range of possible research that can be done with 1990 census data is a huge task; I have hit only a few highlights here. Anyone planning to use census data must be prepared for a fairly large time investment in learning a new vocabulary of geographic, population, and housing terms. Understanding and applying census sampling concepts, making decisions about nonsampling errors and the undercount, and learning to use new technologies (such as CD-ROMs or Geographic Information Systems) can also be a daunting task.

Yet given all this, the decennial census (in conjunction with the large-scale sample surveys conducted by the U.S. government) remains the most important source of information we have about the U.S. population. One need not be an expert in all aspects of the census in order to make intelligent use of many parts of it, and much of the time the advice of specialists is not required. A willingness to read data and definitions carefully, to take advantage of the many recent breakthroughs in information processing, and to pick up the phone and call Bureau of the Census or State Data Center experts for information will be enough to solve the problems most researchers will typically encounter.

References

Advisory Committee on Problems of Census Enumeration [National Research Council]. (1972). *America's uncounted people*. Washington, DC: National Academy of Sciences.

Alonso, W., & Starr, P. (Eds.). (1987). *The politics of numbers*. New York: Russell Sage.

American Demographics staff. (1989). The 1990 Census questionnaire. *American Demographics, 11*(4), 24-31.

Anderson, M. (1988). *The American census: A social history*. New Haven, CT: Yale University Press.

Bates, N. (1993, March). *The 1992 Simplified Questionnaire Test: The item nonresponse and telephone debriefing evaluations*. Paper presented at the 1993 Annual Research Conference, U.S. Bureau of the Census, Arlington, VA.

Beresford, J. (1993, January/February). Year 2000 census planning proceeds in stages. *Association of Public Data Users [APDU] Newsletter Supplement*.

Bogue, D. J. (1985). *The population of the United States: Historical trends and future projections*. New York: Free Press.

Campbell, C. (1993). 1990 census public use microdata samples (PUMS). *Inter-University Consortium for Political and Social Research [ICPSR] Bulletin, 13*(3), 1-4.

Center for Human Resource Research. (1992). *National Longitudinal Survey [NLS] user's guide, 1992*. Columbus: Ohio State University.

Cherlin, A. (1991a). Census monographs on family, work and money [book review]. *Demography, 28*(2), 201-206.

Cherlin, A. (1991b). *Marriage, divorce, remarriage*. Cambridge, MA: Harvard University Press.

Chicago Fact Book Consortium. (1984). *Local community fact book: Chicago metropolitan area*. Chicago: Chicago Fact Book Consortium.

Cho, L.-J., & Hearn, R. L. (Eds.). (1984). *Censuses of Asia and the Pacific: 1980 round*. Honolulu: East-West Population Institute.

Choldin, H. (in press). *Looking for the last percent: The controversy over census undercounts*. New Brunswick, NJ: Rutgers University Press.

Choldin, H. M., & Logan, J. R. (1991). Census monographs on community growth and change. *Demography, 28*(3), 481-492.

Coleman, J. S. (1993). The rational reconstruction of society. *American Sociological Review, 58*(1), 1-15.

Director announces no adjustment of intercensal estimates. (1993). *Association of Public Data Users [APDU] Newsletter, 17*(1), 1, 12.

Eriksen, E. P., Estrada, L. F., Tukey, J. W., & Wolter, K. M. (1991, June 21). *Report on the 1990 decennial census and the Post-Enumeration Survey*. Submitted to the Secretary of the U.S. Department of Commerce.

Fay, R. E., & Thompson. J. (1993, March). *The 1990 Post Enumeration Survey: Statistical lessons, in hindsight*. Paper presented at the Annual Research Conference, U.S. Bureau of the Census, Arlington, VA.

83

Frankfort-Nachmias, C., & Nachmias, D. (1992). *Research methods in the social sciences*. New York: St. Martin's.

Garson, G. D., & Biggs, R. S. (1992). *Analytic mapping and geographic databases*. Newbury Park, CA: Sage.

Goldscheider, C. (1991). Census monographs on ethnicity [book review]. *Demography, 28*(4), 661-666.

Goldscheider, F. K. (1991). Census monographs on family, work and money [book review]. *Demography, 28*(2), 206-211.

Halacy, D. (1980). *Census: 190 years of counting America*. New York: Elsevier/Nelson.

Hessler, R. M. (1992). *Social research methods*. St. Paul, MN: West.

Hill, M. S. (1992). *The Panel Study of Income Dynamics: A user's guide*. Newbury Park, CA: Sage.

Hogan, H. (1993). The 1990 Post-Enumeration Survey: Operations and results. *Journal of the American Statistical Association, 88*(423), 1047-1057.

Hunt, M. (1985). *Profiles of social research*. New York: Russell Sage.

Ihlanfeldt, K. R., & Sjoquist, D. L. (1990). Job accessibility and racial differences in youth unemployment rates. *American Economic Review, 80*(1), 267-276.

Iverson, G. R. (1991). *Contextual analysis*. Newbury Park, CA: Sage.

Jencks, C. (1991). Is the American underclass growing? In C. Jencks & P. E. Peterson (Eds.), *The urban underclass* (pp. 28-102). Washington, DC: Brookings Institution.

Kaplan, C. P., Van Valey, T., & associates. (1980). *Census '80: Continuing the factfinder tradition*. Washington, DC: Government Printing Office.

Landale, N. S., & Tolnay, S. E. (1993). Generation, ethnicity and marriage: Historical patterns in the northern United States. *Demography, 30*(1), 103-126.

Lee, B. A., & Wood, P. B. (1991). Is neighborhood racial succession place-specific? *Demography, 28*(1), 21-40.

Levy, F. (1987). *Dollars and dreams*. New York: Norton.

Marx, R. W. (1990). *Census geography*. Alexandria, VA: American Chamber of Commerce Researchers Association.

Massey, D. (1990). American apartheid: Segregation and the making of the underclass. *American Journal of Sociology, 96*(2), 329-357.

Ministry of Construction. (1986). *Diyici quanguo chengzhen fangwu pucha shougong huizong ziliao huibian* [The results of hand tabulation of the First Housing Census of China]. Beijing: Ministry of Construction of the People's Republic of China.

Mitroff, I. I., Mason, R. O., & Barabba, V. P. (1983). *The 1980 census: Policymaking amid turbulence*. Lexington, MA: D. C. Heath.

Moore, M., & O'Connell, M. (1978). *Perspectives on American fertility* (U.S. Bureau of the Census, Current Population Reports, Special Studies, Series P-23, No. 70). Washington, DC: Government Printing Office.

Murray, M. P. (1992). Census adjustment and the distribution of federal spending. *Demography, 29*(3), 319-332.

Myers, D. (1992). *Analysis with local census data: Portraits of change*. Boston: Academic Press.

Passel, J. S. (1993). Comment. *Journal of the American Statistical Association, 88*(423), 1074-1077.

Raymondo, J. C. (1992). *Population estimation and projection: Methods for marketing, demographic and planning personnel*. New York: Quorum.

Robinson, J. G., Ahmed, B., Gupta, P. D., & Woodrow, K. A. (1993). Estimation of population coverage in the 1990 United States Census based on Demographic Analysis. *Journal of the American Statistical Association, 88*(423), 1061-1079.

84

Schenker, N. (1993). Undercount in the 1990 census. *Journal of the American Statistical Association, 88*(423), 1044-1046.

Scott, A. H. (1968). *Census, U.S.A.: Fact-finding for the American people, 1790-1970.* New York: Seabury.

Starr, P. (1987). The sociology of official statistics. In W. Alonso & P. Starr (Eds.), *The politics of numbers* (pp. 7-58). New York: Russell Sage.

Stevens, G. (1992). The social and demographic context of language use in the U.S. *American Sociological Review, 57*(2), 171-185.

Sweet, J. A., & Bumpass, L. L. (1987). *America's families and households.* New York: Russell Sage.

U.S. Bureau of the Census. (n.d.). *CD-ROM* [compact disk—read only memory] technical information. Washington, DC: U.S. Department of Commerce, Bureau of the Census.

U.S. Bureau of the Census. (1975). *Historical statistics of the United States: Colonial times to 1970.* Washington, DC: Government Printing Office.

U.S. Bureau of the Census. (1983). *Census of population and housing: Public use microdata samples, technical documentation.* Washington, DC: U.S. Department of Commerce, Bureau of the Census.

U.S. Bureau of the Census. (1988). *1980 Census of population and housing. Evaluation and research reports. The coverage of population in the 1980 Census. PHC80-E4.* Washington, DC: U.S. Department of Commerce, Bureau of the Census.

U.S. Bureau of the Census. (1989). *The relationship between the 1970 and 1980 industry and occupation classification systems* (Technical Paper No. 59). Washington, DC: U.S. Department of Commerce, Bureau of the Census.

U.S. Bureau of the Census. (1991). *1990 Census of Population and Housing. Summary Tape File 1. Technical Documentation.* Washington, DC: U.S. Department of Commerce, Bureau of the Census.

U.S. Bureau of the Census. (1992a). *General population characteristics, 1990* [various states]. Washington, DC: Government Printing Office.

U.S. Bureau of the Census. (1992b). *Geographic tabulation entities* [mimeographed, rev. December 1992]. Washington, DC: U.S. Department of Commerce, Bureau of the Census, Geography Division.

U.S. Bureau of the Census. (1992c). *Income, poverty and wealth in the United States: A chartbook.* Current Population Reports, Series P-60, No. 179. Washington, DC: Government Printing Office.

U.S. Bureau of the Census. (1992d). *Maps and more: Your guide to Census Bureau geography.* Washington, DC: U.S. Department of Commerce, Bureau of the Census.

U.S. Bureau of the Census. (1992e). *1990 Census of Population and Housing: Guide. Part A. Text.* Washington, DC: Government Printing Office.

U.S. Bureau of the Census. (1992f). *1990 Census of Population and Housing: Public use microdata samples: United States, technical documentation.* Washington, DC: U.S. Department of Commerce, Bureau of the Census.

U.S. Bureau of the Census. (1992g). *Population trends in the 1980's.* Current Population Reports, Series P23, No. 175. Washington, DC: Government Printing Office.

U.S. Bureau of the Census. (1992h). *Statistical abstract of the United States: 1992.* Washington, DC: Government Printing Office.

U.S. Bureau of the Census. (1992i). *Summary social, economic and housing characteristics, 1990* [various states]. Washington, DC: Government Printing Office.

U.S. Bureau of the Census. (1993a). *A guide to state and local census geography.* Washington, DC: U.S. Department of Commerce, Bureau of the Census.

U.S. Bureau of the Census. (1993b). *1980 industry and occupation categories that had title or code changes for the 1990 Census of Population* (Mimeo, 27 May 1992; revised 18 August 1993). Washington, DC: U.S. Department of Commerce, Bureau of the Census.

U.S. Bureau of the Census. (1993c). *1990 Census of population and housing: Part B. Glossary.* Washington, DC: Government Printing Office.

U.S. General Accounting Office. (1991a). *Formula programs: Adjusted census data would redistribute small percentage of funds to states* [GAO/GDD-92-12, 7 November 1991]. Washington, DC: U.S. General Accounting Office.

U.S. General Accounting Office. (1991b). *1990 census: Reported net undercount obscured magnitude of error* [GAO/GDD-91-113, 22 August 1991). Washington, DC: U.S. General Accounting Office.

U.S. General Accounting Office. (1992). *Decennial census: 1990 results show need for fundamental reform* [GAO/GDD-92-94, 9 June 1992]. Washington, DC: U. S. General Accounting Office.

Wilson, W. J. (1987). *The truly disadvantaged: The inner city, the underclass, and public policy.* Chicago: University of Chicago Press.

Yaukey, D. (1985). *Demography: The study of human population.* New York: St. Martin's.

About the Author

Richard E. Barrett is Associate Professor of Sociology and Adjunct Associate Professor of Epidemiology and Biostatistics at the University of Illinois at Chicago. His research interests span demography, social organization, and social epidemiology in China and the United States and have included such topics as share tenancy, dependency theory, seasonality of vital rates, labor force participation, bastardy, and changes in uterine cancer rates. His work has been published in *American Journal of Sociology, Demography, Economic Development and Cultural Change, American Journal of Public Health, American Sociological Review,* and *New England Journal of Medicine.*

His current research includes projects on social change in 10 counties in China since 1979, the contribution of government employment to African American economic progress, hepatitis B incidence and prevention in China and the United States, and how changing sex ratios have affected marriage markets in China since 1950.